Son Glasses

A True Story
Walking by Faith, Not by Sight

A biography of: Ron Barton

Biographer: Michael Wolff

SON GLASSES: A TRUE STORY
WALKING BY FAITH, NOT BY SIGHT BY RON BARTON
Published by American Publishing

ISBN: 978-1-965649-01-5
Copyright © 2024 by Ron Barton
Cover design by Elaina Lee, For the Muse Design, forthemusedesign.com
Interior design by atritex.com

Available in print from your local bookstore, online, or from the publisher.

All scripture quotations, unless otherwise indicated, are taken from the Holy Bible, New International Version®, NIV®. Copyright ©1973, 1978, 1984, 2011 by Biblica, Inc.TM. Used by permission of Zondervan. All rights reserved worldwide. www.zondervan.com. "NIV" and "New International Version" are trademarks registered in the United States Patent and Trademark Office by Biblica, Inc.TM.

Library of Congress Cataloging-in-Publication Data
Barton, Ron.
Son Glasses: A True Story. Walking by Faith, Not by Sight / Ron Barton
1st ed.

Printed in the United States of America

ENDORSEMENTS:

Ron Barton is an inspiration to everyone who knows him. His story will lift your spirit and encourage you to live a better life. I am thankful for his friendship and for the full story of his life that he tells in this book. You will be too!

Bo Mitchell
MLB and NBA Chaplain
Author of *Grace Behind Bars*, Denver, Colorado

This is a book of hope, telling the story of a man accomplishing what many would consider impossible. It will encourage you to up your game with the Lord, or to start one, no matter where you may be on that timeline. Ron Barton has experienced the pain, the joy, and everything in between, and he will share with you how you can accept the challenges and thrive through all of them.

Evangelist William Fay
Author of *Sharing Jesus Without Fear*, Denver, Colorado

The quote from Ron that sticks with me is "I had been blind all my life, and it took the loss of my eyesight before I could truly see. Losing my sight from a mugging was a blessing in disguise because it led me to accept Christ into my life."

I have known Ron over the past 20+ years and consider him a one-of-a-kind friend. He impressed me the first time we met, as I piloted his tandem, that there was no obstacle he could not conquer. He considers adversity as just another opportunity to share his deeply held beliefs in God's grace, provision, and strength. His story demonstrates how these beliefs have allowed

him to overcome adversity throughout his life. He not only tells everyone he meets what he believes, he LIVES what he believes!

Nathan Dick
Friend and Tandem Pilot, Estes Park, Colorado

When asked to write Ron's story, I had no idea what I was about to encounter. It is rare to know anyone with a disability who has lived the full life he has. Certainly, I have not. This is a man who overcomes trials, tribulations, and disabilities with astonishing purpose and enduring quality. It is this story that has led to the pages of this book. The relationships he has formed all around the world, the lives he has touched with his fierce determination to use what should have undone him to evangelize others, and the many accomplishments that have marked his life will encourage and strengthen you no matter how formidable your situation may seem. Stories like Ron's will make you rise up, believe once again in your God and yourself, and overcome!

Michael Wolff
Author/Biographer
Director of Reconnections Ministries, Englewood, Colorado

"God loves you just the way you are,
but he refuses to leave you that way.
He wants you to be just like Jesus."
– Max Lucado

TABLE OF CONTENTS

Chapter I:

LIFE BEFORE CHRIST—
THE EARLY YEARS

Mugged!

It was April 1975, and I was working for Kyburz Construction Company in Limon, Colorado. We had just finished building the Cottonwood Care Center. My boss and I, and one other employee, went to a local bar to have a drink and say goodbye to that dust speck of a town on the windy eastern Colorado plains.

At another table were nine members of the Burlington Chapter of the Junior Chamber of Commerce Civic Organization (the Jaycees) getting drunk and rowdy. They had been at a joint meeting with the Limon Chapter before coming to the bar, having already polished off a quart of Kentucky Bourbon on the way. These boys were feeling good and looking for trouble, so they targeted one of my friends with long blond hair, threatening to shave it off for him. Sensing trouble was brewing, the bar manager came over and asked them to leave.

My group decided to go to another establishment because their harassment had left a sour taste in our mouths. However, the Jaycees, with gang mentality, were now firmly in control, and they were not finished with us. When we left the bar, I walked up the street a bit to get my motorcycle. When I returned, I noticed my boss and one of our friends trying to resecure his bike in the back of his pickup. Our tormentors had cut all the ropes that had it tied down, and they were waiting for us. When I started helping my friends with the bike, all nine of them jumped on us! The guy who had cut the ropes was wielding his knife and began cutting the ropes we had just tied. As he was doing that, another one of them started throwing punches at me, trying to get me to fight him.

For once in my life (see Family and Friends), I did the smart thing. Knowing it would be stupid for the three of us to take on nine drunks, with one holding a knife, I did not fight back. I just tried to do my best to ward off the blows with my motorcycle helmet. Nevertheless, one of those punches got through and hit me hard in the face. I was wearing wire-rimmed glasses at the time, and the punch broke the nose bridge on the glasses, which exposed a wire that pierced and ruptured my right eyeball. Inasmuch as my left eye had always been the weakest and of little good, without my right eye, my world was plunged into darkness!

I instantly cried out in pain, then shock, then anguish. "I can't see! I can't see!" My friends sat me down on a curb, and I just kept repeating the mantra, "I'm blind! Help! I can't see!" All I could think was that I would never be able to see again. After all my former close brushes with total blindness, this one felt real and final. It would be an understatement to say I was in a state of total shock, depression, and hopelessness. Wasn't it bad enough that I had been born with seriously limited vision? Did my eyes need to be constantly injured to make things even worse? Little did I know God had a plan for a total makeover of my life—or should I say learning to "walk by faith, not by sight" through these very afflictions in my life.

When our tormentors saw they had seriously injured me, they got scared, got back in their cars, and took off. After so many incidents where I had been the perpetrator (you will read about that in the pages to come), I was now the victim. The police were called, a report was filed, and officers were sent after the guys who attacked us. Fortunately, the president of the Limon Chapter of the Jaycees had witnessed the attack and identified them to the police.

My friends put me in a car and took me to the Denver University Hospital Emergency, where I spent the whole night waiting to get checked in and wondering anew if I had seen my last light of day. The next morning several ophthalmologists came to examine my right eye. Then a retinal specialist was called, who moved me to Saint Luke's Hospital. There I would undergo laser treatments which, temporarily, gave me partial sight in that eye. I was no stranger to partial vision, so at least there was hope. The story of my blindness, how that affected my mental state and my life, and the circumstances leading up to the decision that would forever change me will be the subject of the rest of this chapter.

Life on the Farm

Born in 1948 in Washington State, I had four brothers and four sisters. We lived on an 80-acre parcel of land my dad had purchased to fulfill his dream of having a farm and a dairy. One of the benefits of this property was a creek that ran through the middle of it, which we used to irrigate the crops. It doubled as a recreational retreat from the scorching summer days spent hauling heavy bales of hay. Mom and Dad did the best they could, providing for a family of eleven in a small three-bedroom home on a very tight budget, but that was the price of a dream.

By the time I was three years old, my parents suspected something was wrong because I kept running into walls and tripping, so they took me to the family doctor. The diagnosis came back that my eyesight was so poor that I was considered legally blind. Back in that day, the only solution was what was known as "Coke-bottle" glasses, the name earned due to the super-thick lenses. And while they made life bearable, my appearance haunted me throughout my early school years. Everyone called me "Four Eyes" and other names that made me feel like some kind of circus freak. Other fallout from my vision problems included being held back in elementary school because I was such a slow reader and had trouble seeing the chalkboard during classes.

There was always work to do around the farm, and as my siblings and I grew, our large family made quite the work crew! The summers were filled with never-ending growing, cutting, baling, hauling, stacking, and storing of hay. The year-round work never ended, and we would have to pitch in the moment we got home from school, and most weekends as well. This made for little or no social life, and though I had a few close male friends, ol' Four Eyes never had much interaction with girls, for obvious reasons.

My first love with a girl named Caren. She was one of the Brown triplet girls. Although we were only in the third grade, I proposed to her! Needless to say, experiencing a crush on a member of the opposite sex at such a young age, I had no idea what to do with my runaway emotions. She was not so unsure, and when I presented my symbolic ring to her on bended knee, she turned me down flat. My crush on Caren continued all the way through high school. This was just the first of a series of rejections I would suffer, primarily due to my poor vision. As time went on, I became increasingly introverted and very insecure around girls.

Do not get me wrong, apart from my vision problems, life growing up on the farm had its upside. My siblings and I, at one time or another, were all members of the 4-H Club, raising our own calves for the stock shows. It was a lot of hard work, but the benefits were pretty cool if you could raise a grand champion. And besides, we got time off from school to prepare for shows and for the events themselves. This opportunity only came around once per year, and we all really looked forward to it.

Trouble Brewing

The earliest indication that I would grow up to be a troublemaker was in 1953, at the age of five, when my younger brother and I nearly burned down the Barton farmhouse. We had a potbellied stove that sat in the middle of the living room, and we took rolled-up newspapers to make torches so we could run around with the lights off, waving them in the dark. One day, the flames got a little bit out of control and switching roles from arsonists to firemen, my brother tried to put the burning paper out by shoving his torch between the mattresses in the bed to smother the flame. I threw mine under the sink in the bathroom. (Note: I did not say under the *faucet* in the bathroom but under the *sink*). Brilliance is a learned attribute. Our efforts led to a ruined box spring and mattress in the bedroom, and a fire in the bathroom.

When my mother heard the smoke alarms we had set off, she came running from the barn to put out the fire. While she was successful initially, we came to find out that the walls of our ancient home were filled with sawdust insulation, a standard practice at the time. Apparently, the sawdust had been sparked, and it smoldered for several weeks before it finally ignited and started the fire all over again. This time, what we had started ignited into a full-blown fire, and the whole house burned down along with most of our possessions.

It was then we realized another wonderful aspect of life on the farm in a small town, as our neighbors and some relatives all pitched in and built us a brand-new house that was larger and included much-needed space for the Barton clan. I doubt such unselfish community support would have happened in the big city, even back in those kinder, gentler days. However, that did not stop hell's fury in the form of work and more work from landing squarely on the two young troublemakers who started the fires to begin with.

Later, when I was in seventh grade, there was a little grocery store one block from the junior high school. I spent a lot of time at that store during the lunch hour, where I found myself moving from perusing the fast-food aisles and soft-drink machines to spending way too much time in the magazine aisle with the skin magazines. You know, the ones behind the cleverly designed covers that leave just enough revealed so as to make the cover irrelevant? Out of all my addictions, and there were plenty, this became one of the worst and one that would haunt me for years.

You can imagine a kid like me, with little or no hope of forming a connection with the opposite sex in the real world, diving into the fantasy world of pornography with both feet. All I ever got out of it was a false interpretation of what love was. Fortunately, after I came to know Jesus Christ, met the woman He had chosen especially for me, and finally learned the meaning of true love, that temptation left me. I now count myself blessed because I know many men who spend their entire lives under bondage to that evil.

That is not the only trouble I got into in stores. In the early '60s, I spent several weeks in Spokane with my aunt and uncle and cousins. As if I did not have enough vices at the time, while I was there, one of their neighbor kids got us all into shoplifting. One of my cousins was wheelchair-bound due to polio. We would go into the stores pushing the wheelchair and swipe whatever we wanted, hiding it behind his back or under his butt. Who, after all, would bust a poor kid in a wheelchair?

However, because we frequented one store too often without ever buying anything, we drew a lot of suspicion. The store security guard made us his priority one day. We were thinking we had this thing down, and having become quite brazen in our approach, we were easily observed and apprehended. Once again, we got off easy with the law because my aunt and uncle paid for everything. However, we did not get off so lightly with my parents.

Then came the day on the school bus when I had had enough of the bullying and harassment over my limited eyesight. The driver was part of a local family with several children who rode on my route. One of the fathers in the clan was a boxer who had taught his kids how to fight. One of his sons loved to bully other kids because of his boxing skills, and so he was constantly getting in fights at school. He was also one of the tormentors constantly ribbing me—egging me on so I would engage with him.

One afternoon, riding home on that bus, he finally got his wish. He was sitting in the seat behind me and kept making fun of me. I turned around, jumped over the seat, and put him into a headlock. Once I had him there, trapping his fists, I started banging his head against the back of the seat in front of us. His cousin, sitting nearby, ripped my coat trying to pull me off of him, but I was not to be denied. Not that day. This was the beating he and everyone who had ever made fun of me at school had coming for a long time, and it was sweet revenge. I kept up the beating until his uncle, who drove the bus, separated us! It was kind of scary, the anger and hatred I was capable of when people pushed the right buttons.

Inasmuch as this kid's uncle was the bus driver, he did not want to hear about the constant taunting. I am sure the cousin painted a picture of the incident as the crazy blind kid going postal for no reason at all. It was a family gang frame-up. I got suspended from riding the bus for a couple of weeks, and once again I was in the doghouse with my folks. Being hard-working, strong, quiet types, discipline came in the form of consequences more than words. With plenty of demanding work always available around the farm, there was never a shortage of consequences to dole out.

Reckless Driving

Even though my parents prohibited me from having a driver's license, due to my choices and poor vision, I still was able to do a lot of driving around our farm and to other farms nearby, as long as I stayed off the main roads. I was twenty-one years old before I obtained a license to legally drive. Having to wait for my license did not help my emotional state, as that is what most fifteen-year-olds look forward to more than any other thing, except perhaps being old enough to drink. All of the friends I had grown up with were getting their licenses, and once again, I was the outsider. The saving grace was my younger brother, Roger. He and I were very close, and after he got his license, transportation was not that much of a problem. He always invited me to come along with him whenever he went somewhere. I knew I could count on him if I really needed a ride.

Two teenagers just cruising through the countryside with nothing better to do. What could go wrong? Plenty. There was the day we found a case of dynamite and decided to employ it to blow up mailboxes. Not satisfied with that level of destruction, we advanced to a few old, abandoned homes in the area. We did not realize that blowing up mailboxes is a federal offense—let alone blowing up an abandoned home! The county probably silently applauded. However, these actions can put your face squarely on the post office wall. Someone who recognized Roger's vehicle around the explosions and smoke reported us to the police.

Talk about freaked out! When the cops showed up at school, we were invited into the principal's office, one by one, to be told exactly what charges we were facing! Fortunately, seeing we were just kids with too much time on our hands and far too little sense, they let us go with a warning. However, that did not exclude our parents from having to reimburse the city for the fragmented mailboxes. I think they figured we did the city a favor by demolishing those old, broken-down houses, but someone had to pay for those old mailboxes. Go figure.

Some of us mixed our demolition exploits with a truly dangerous game of chicken. As we drove along the road, we would light the fuse on a stick of dynamite, wait until it was almost at the cap, and then throw the stick out the window just before it went off. These were not the cherry bombs or M-80s most kids play with on the Fourth of July that might take out your eyes, ears, or a few fingers, mind you. These were whole sticks of dynamite that could blow the car and everyone in it to kingdom come with just one slipup! However, this is what these farm kids, with a feeling of immortality and a lust for adventure, did with their spare time.

Mom and Dad

With all that work to do to make ends meet, discipline around the farm was never lacking. I learned at an early age never to sass my parents, especially my mother. One time, I let my mouth follow my thoughts a little too closely and without restraint, and

I ended up running for my life from my broom-wielding mother! My parents were good people who loved us a lot, but there was just too much to be done for us to be fooling around and giving them a hard time.

Dad and Mom were beloved by most of our friends, even the young ones. When I graduated from high school, Dad bought a pool table and set it up in the basement. Several of our friends would come out to the house to challenge him. He loved pool, and also joined us in spirited baseball games. It was a standing joke in the family that he raised his own baseball team. When we played, it was the Bartons against all comers. You could say we were a family that knew how to work and play together.

Some of my best friends even moved out to the farm, which they paid for in blood, sweat, and tears working the hay bales. Mom and Dad offered to pay them, but all they would accept was the beer Mom kept readily on hand. My dad never had to hire anyone around the farm because of the army of free labor provided by family and friends. It is pretty cool when most of your friends call your parents "Mom and Dad." I think they were some of the most familiar, loved, and respected people in all of Colville.

I never knew if my father was counting on one of us boys to take over the family farm because we really never talked about it. I was not sure if that was because of my constant problems with my eyesight or my rebellious attitude, but there were several times my dad let me know that I would never amount to anything, so why would he want me to take over anyway? I have never considered myself anything but fortunate to have the parents I had, but nobody is perfect.

Adding Insult to Injury

Unloading a hay truck during one of those summer days in 1959, I suffered a critical eye injury. My older brother Roy Lee was trying to force me to unload the truck by myself. When I flatly refused, he threw a rock that hit me in the head. This resulted in a retinal detachment in my left eye. Great, I thought, why did that rock have to hit me in the head and not somewhere else? My folks did not have any medical insurance at the time. Still, when my mother was told the prognosis, she researched experimental laser treatments being done at the University of Oregon. She signed me up, desperate for any help in restoring what was left of my eyesight. Unfortunately, the treatments were in the early years of development and proved unsuccessful. Because I was just eleven years old and facing such unknowns, this outcome was hard to wrap my head around and harder yet to accept. I had no idea how my current crisis was going to affect the rest of my life, and my tendency was to believe the worst.

After that, I became known at school as the kid who was blind in one eye and could not see out of the other. This made me even more insecure and turned me into a total introvert who did very little socializing with anybody—a lifestyle that endured all the way through high school. Kids who have Down Syndrome or autism are not treated nearly as harshly as those who are fat, unattractive, or walk around wearing Coke-bottle lenses on their noses like I did. Being treated every day in the cruelest sort of way, like I was some sort of freak, took a toll on me. With my poor vision, contact sports were out of the question, there was no social calendar, keeping up in class was difficult because everything was on a chalkboard that I could not see, friendships were sparse, and dating? Really? It all led to me, along with my brothers and a few friends, constantly pushing the envelope of sensible behavior, seeing just how far we could take our actions without getting in serious trouble with our parents or the law. It is nearly impossible for me to explain to someone else how being the butt of jokes and feeling like an outcast during my formative years in school affected me.

Above-the-neck trauma happened again as I turned seventeen. My dad was building a new milking parlor and had scaffolding set up around most of it. Because I only had sight in one eye, I was constantly running into the scaffolding with my head. You guessed it: this caused another retinal detachment in my one barely normal eye. I missed almost half of my sophomore year in high school after retinal surgery and months of recovery in San Francisco. Years later, that old barn served as a notice to all the world that this was the Barton farm because my patriotic sister painted it red, white, and blue. This was to honor my two brothers who served as Marines in the military.

My struggles in school continued until I reached my senior year, when I discovered that I was pretty good at math. I did not have long reading assignments, as was the case with other classes; I just had to understand the lessons. Word of my proficiency spread as other students in my class came to me for help when they had math problems. I took a bookkeeping class and realized this could be an occupation to shoot for. For the first time in my life, I got serious about school and brought my grade point average up so I could actually qualify for college. I decided that I wanted to major in business and minor in accounting to become a CPA. It gave me hope that my schooling would count for something and that I would not have to be a dairy farmer for the rest of my life.

Off to College

When I pursued an accounting degree at Eastern Washington State University in 1968, school policy dictated that I had to live in a dorm. This was my first real taste of anything resembling a social life. I initially tried to focus on my studies, but there was significant partying going on in the meantime. Combining partying with studying for finals led us to pop a lot of over-the-counter energy pills and speed. Where were the energy drinks so many young people are hooked on today back then when I needed them? Anyway, my grades reflected my lifestyle and were far from acceptable back home.

Then, early in my second year, my dorm buddies and I moved into a rented house in Spokane, about twenty miles off campus. After the first quarter of that year, things took a turn for the worse as the college-life-good-times bug started to seriously bite. Our new abode afforded us a lifestyle change: forget your studies, skip classes, and party down with the boys!

While I was certainly not a perfect child prior to my college years, I never drank, took drugs, or smoked cigarettes. However, if you wanted to fit in with the college party group, you had to get involved in all of that. When you have been the outcast all your life and never fit in with anyone, you cannot imagine the pressure you put on yourself to see things change. The lure, even if it is for all the wrong reasons, was overwhelming.

When the Jesus Revolution reached Colville, I had one of my first real encounters with Christians. It threatened to interrupt the parties, and I wanted nothing to do with "them." These so-called "Jesus freaks" confronted me, telling me how much God loved me. I always responded, "If God really loves me, how could He allow my life to suck so bad? How could a loving God create me with such poor eyesight, the butt of jokes in school all my life, a freak to the girls I wanted to ask for a date, and the only guy at my school without a driver's license? He loves me? Gimme a break."

More Trouble

The following year, my brother Roger wanted me to drive his 1964 Oldsmobile 442 Cutlass to the airport. He was going with another friend who owned an identical model Olds, and they were going to race across the nearby flats. It was a chilly night, and there was a lot of frost on the windshield. I turned the defroster on, but I did not wait for it to clear the windshield. I was doing 120 mph when I ran it off the road, through a barbed-wire fence, and through a telephone pole. Yes, I said "through." The first of three loyal steeds to be totaled! A friend, who was riding with me, and I both walked away with minor injuries. The big, heavy sedan had saved us, although we certainly did not return the favor.

It was a sad scene when my brother saw the flashing lights from the police cars and his "baby" sitting in the middle of the road, unrecognizable. I do not remember exactly how I got off the hook for that one. Had I pulled all these shenanigans with the laws being what they are today, I would probably still be in jail. However, the insurance company and the law somehow overlooked that I was driving a car that was not mine, was more than half-blind, and did not have a license! The money Roger received from the insurance company partially paid for a gorgeous new 1969 Road Runner.

Later that summer, a large group of us went to Omak, Washington, to the Omak Stampede. We saw a bit of the rodeo there, but it ended with me marching drunk across a guy's yard with a staff in one hand and a wizard hat on my head, singing "When the Saints Go Marching In." Then I climbed up onto the roof of the doghouse and gave a Sunday morning sermon of pure gibberish that had nothing to do with God or the gospel! I had no idea what I was talking about, but I think perhaps the Lord may have been giving me some insight into where I was eventually headed, sans the doghouse and wizard hat.

Returning from Omak, my brother, inspired by my rooftop sermon, decided we needed to make a grand entrance back into Colville. As we entered the city limits, Roger leaned on his horn all the way down Main Street so everyone could join our party and celebrate the return of two of its favorite sons. Of course, we did not consider that in such a small town the local sheriff might just be taking a break at a local diner as we drove by. Wondering, like everyone else, what all the commotion was about, he jumped into his patrol car and followed us down the street with his flashing lights on. Now that is a grand entrance with a police escort!

When the cop came up to the car door, he asked if we had been drinking, and of course we all said no, but the open bottles of beer sitting in the car behind our backs said otherwise. Busted, we were on our way to the hoosegow. This was my first time in county jail, even though it was far from the first time I had deserved it. Our parents were called, but we had run out of get-out-of-jail-free cards with them. It turns out they were fed up with our shenanigans and decided to let us stew a bit in the pot we had prepared for ourselves.

We spent the entire weekend as guests of the Stevens County Jail. It was bad enough word got around we were incarcerated, but they gave us buzz cuts as well. My beautiful locks, once down around my shoulders, now lay in a useless pile on the floor. This incident would be a harbinger of trouble with the authorities for years to come.

Never letting a thing like jail time deter us, we kept on partying. "When the cat's away," as they say. My parents left town on a salmon fishing trip with my uncle on the first vacation I had ever known them to take. So, we decided to have a three-day kegger. Oh, we justified the event by making it a fundraiser to buy carpet for the home the neighbors helped us build.

One of the nights, we got a call from someone who had left the party early, informing us the sheriff, who had previously clipped my hair, was headed in our direction. I hated that man for playing barber with me, and so I grabbed my rifle and lay down in a ditch to ambush him. I was so drunk and angry I was really going to shoot a police officer! Looking back on it later, I knew God was watching over me that night, even though I wanted nothing to do with Him. I was so drunk that I passed out, and Roger came and took the rifle away from me. The sheriff never even showed up, and I escaped being one of the prison lifers I minister to today.

Off to Work

I had had enough of college, and the lie I was living, wherein I believed I had the world by the tail; but the facts revealed a very different picture, and so I dropped out in 1970. It was then I started climbing the corporate ladder at Avey Brothers Sawmill to where I could perform any function except operating the big bandsaws, and I wanted no part of them anyway. While working there on the evening swing shift, I also started working in the daytime for a friend named Greg, who was running a construction crew there in Colville. Greg was going through a divorce at the time, so I moved into his house with him and one other guy, where the partying never stopped.

For fun during the summers, we would float down the Kettle River near the Canadian border carrying a half-case of beer in our laps. The biggest challenge was to run the rapids without losing any of our precious brews, much less getting tossed out of our tubes onto the large rocks that bordered both sides. This sort of activity struck me as particularly stupid for a guy who was inclined to losing more and more of his eyesight bumping into things, but I had never been known as one who looked before he leaped.

During the winters, most of my friends were turning to skiing for recreation, and they finally convinced me to join them. The guy with little or no eyesight barreling down a hill where people with perfect vision had trouble seeing all the hazards? I repeat, I had never been known as one who looked before he leaped. Somehow, I survived both the rapids and the slopes. With the help of some terrific ski guides, I became a good skier after I totally lost my eyesight. I enjoy the sport to this day.

In the winter of 1971, after I finally obtained a driver's license, some critical equipment at Avey Brothers went down, and we were laid off for several months. During that time, a friend of mine and I decided to take a trip to Colorado, and then from Colorado, go north through Wyoming to Miles City, Montana, to visit some other friends who had moved there from Colville.

On the way through Wyoming, my car started having serious health issues, and it finally gave up the ghost. I found a Hot Rod 1970 Barracuda to replace it for a measly $3,200, thanks to a cosign on the loan from my parents. Oh, to have that car back today! Good examples are worth six figures at auction now. After spending a few weeks traveling, we ran out of money and places to stay, so we decided to head back home to Colville. Shortly after our return, I hit a deer and wrecked the 'Cuda.

Accidents on the road just seemed to follow me, and shortly after that, I hit another deer on my Honda motorcycle, going about 60 mph. The deer wrapped around the side of the bike and smashed my leg into the tailpipe. My faithful Honda and I survived, unfortunately, the deer did not. However, my road travails were not over. Shortly after that, I got hit head-on by a car that crossed into my lane, and my bike did not survive that one. If you are keeping score, that is two dead deer, one telephone-impaled and totaled Olds, one deer-impaled and wrecked 'Cuda, and one totaled Honda motorcycle—but I was still alive and kicking! The incident that destroyed my bike was the second time I should have been killed, or at least seriously maimed, but once again I walked away with nary a scratch.

Ron and his Honda

Back to epic parties. In July of 1971, my buddies drove a classic VW van painted in psychedelic colors to the Universal Life Church Picnic over the Fourth of July weekend. This "picnic" lasted several days in Idaho at the Farragut State Park and was anything but a church gathering. It later became known as the Idaho Hippie Festival. Good touch, our van. This flower-power counterculture revolution had become a drug-saturated, free-love-fueled rock festival. So much for Idaho's innocence bubble, which was irreparably ruptured.

It did not take the park agents and local police too long to get wind of the event, and they figured out Aunt May and Granny Ethel were not attending a church gathering with their picnic basket to donate to Yogi Bear. Shocked by naked, drugged-out hippies dancing throughout the park, local officials begged the state to deny future permits, but at that time, by law, a church had every right to gather on state land. And so the event was allowed to go on, no one knowing what the collateral damage would be. It came to be known as Idaho's Woodstock Festival, with some sources estimating that somewhere between 20,000 and 40,000 people were in attendance.

During the fall of the following year, I had been drinking pretty heavily at my rented house when I ran out of beer. I decided to drive to the liquor store to get another case, and as I shot out of the driveway onto the highway, I overcorrected my turn and did a complete one-eighty, ending up in a ditch. Another encounter with my favorite sheriff's department and my third stay in the Stevens County jail—this time with a DUI and a suspended driver's license tacked on. Roger came to rescue my car from the ditch, but this country boy's luck had run out, and no one was turning up any longer to rescue me from my own foolishness.

In 1973, when I was renting a house that became marijuana central, I began collecting a lot of the seeds from my friends, which I kept in my dresser drawer, in hopes that one day we could grow our own on the acreage there. We finally convinced my brother Roy Lee, who happened to have somewhat of a green thumb, to attempt to grow our first crop. When my landlord asked us what we were growing, we told him potato plants. Yes, sometimes ignorance is bliss.

Later, Roy Lee moved in with me and began growing his own crop, but you-know-who ended up spending two months in the Stevens County Jail when we got busted with the plants. I will never forget the day a number of police officers pulled into Avey Brothers, and I watched one of the cops go into the office. A few minutes later, my boss and the officer walked out toward the sorter where I was working, and you can guess the rest. This only served to make me increasingly angry and rebellious, because I did not understand why my brother received half the time in the hoosegow that I received when they were his plants!

Though Roy Lee eventually went to the sheriff and confessed they were his plants, the cops found the bag of marijuana seeds I had been collecting in my dresser drawer when they searched the place. So, considering that my name was on the lease, they were not about to let me slide. Again, I got the worst of it, but upon reflection, I considered it somewhat of a lifetime achievement award because I had certainly gained a reputation with the local authorities. Fortunately, one of the Avey brothers decided he could not live without us, and he got us out of jail on a work-release program. At least that gave us freedom during working hours.

It is funny how times change. If I went before a judge today with the same offenses, they would permanently revoke my driver's license, put me in jail, and throw away the key. However, if they found marijuana on my property in many states today, it would not be a big deal. All in all, I got off pretty easy, considering my history.

Change of Scenery

As comfortable and cheap as I was living, I knew it would not do to stay in Colville any longer after I got out of jail. Nothing I was trying to do in my hometown was working to pull me out of the cycle of partying, getting in trouble, and going nowhere in life. I had squandered most of my young life, which began as a kid who had grown up in a loving family with so much to look forward to. I needed to sort through and perhaps gain a clearer perspective on why my life had become such a train wreck. I had been evicted from the house where we were growing the marijuana plants, so it seemed now was as good a time as any to embark on a new adventure somewhere else.

I began to map out a two-week trip that would take me on a tour of most of the western United States. It would be a four-stop journey ending in Aurora, Colorado, where I would visit my oldest brother, Leslie. As I started out on a new Honda CB350F that was my pride and joy, the sun gleaming off the deep metallic green paint and nothing but my backpack and a sleeping bag attached to the sissy bar behind me, I could not begin to imagine how the journey I was about to take would change my life forever.

After traveling through Wyoming, I stopped for a few days in Aurora to visit with my brother Leslie, before traveling east to Limon to look up some friends I knew from Colville. Leslie and I reminisced about the past and what this trip would hopefully accomplish. My parents considered Leslie a role model who never got into trouble, and he could not understand how they had failed so miserably in my life. He agreed with me that just getting away from my peers in Colville might be the best thing I could do for myself. Yet I was leaving there and heading out to reunite with some of those very same people. Not a terrific start.

When I arrived in Limon, one of my friends took me out one evening to a bar in Hugo, where I met seventeen-year-old Rose. She was drop-dead gorgeous and turned out to be quite a jokester. She could cut you to pieces with her quick wit. She used to say to me, "If your brain was gasoline, you would not have enough to run a pissant's motorcycle around the inside of a Cheerio!" However, as we got to know each other and our relationship grew, she was also not afraid to give me a tough time about how much she saw me drinking, and I respected her for that.

Rose was the most popular girl in Limon at that time. She was a senior in high school, and I was twenty-four. Rose had seven brothers and two younger sisters, and her family immediately adopted me as one of their own. In fact, several of her brothers tried to find employment for me in Limon so that I would move to Colorado permanently. Soon, a meaningful relationship formed between her and me. Perhaps I had grown up somewhat, I thought, because I was not about to make the same mistake that I made with that girl back in the third grade when I proposed to her right away. I might give it a few days this time.

However, the past did not remain in the past, as Rose's brother Kenny and I became fast party friends in what was known as the drug capital of Colorado. If I was not spending time with Rose, I was with Kenny doing all those things that got me in trouble back home. While my original itinerary was shot to hell, I figured a fresh start was what this trip was all about, so I decided to let the chips fall where they may. However, soon the pockets needed lining, and nothing much was coming of my job search there in Limon, so I decided that I had better get back to Colville and my job at the sawmill.

After packing up my Honda and saying my goodbyes, I stopped by a construction site on the outskirts of Limon where Lawrence Construction was building an overpass bridge on I-70. Given my previous construction experience, I was hired on the spot. They asked me to start work the following Monday. Overjoyed that I would not have to leave Limon to have gainful employment, I went back and unpacked. Then, I took a flight back to Washington to pick up a few of my things and let my bosses at Avey know I was leaving for good.

From the Plains to the Mountains

One of the lures that initially brought me to Colorado was my love of skiing, which had begun in Washington. Inasmuch as going to the slopes with skis, boots, and poles was not an option on my motorcycle, I found a foreign compact convertible that I thought would be ideal for what I needed. A rear-wheel drive convertible as a great ski vehicle? Sometimes, I impressed myself with my own brilliance. On my first trip up to the Eisenhower tunnel, I discovered winter-mountain driving was an adventure with such a vehicle even with good tires, and mine were bald! After a trip to the tire store, I finally made it up to Copper Mountain, where I quickly realized this was true skiing, on a much grander scale than back home. I was in awe of the majesty and size of the Rockies, and to this day, Copper is still one of my favorite ski areas.

While my love of the Colorado mountains was only growing, my relationship with Rose ended. In March of 1974, when I thought our relationship was in great shape, I decided to take the big step that I had failed so badly with my third-grade girlfriend, and I proposed to Rose. It was strike two and another failure. I think her mom was probably concerned that a twenty-five-year-old man wanted to wed her eighteen-year-old daughter. However, we broke up for whatever reason, and I took it hard. This relationship with Rose was not third-grade puppy love—this was the real deal for me.

I turned back to my old friend the bottle, and one night at a party, I became unglued when I saw Rose with another guy. I got in my car and decided to push those new tires to the limit. Not only are your reflexes and mental capacities hindered when you drink and drive, but your judgment concerning how drunk you are is likewise impaired. I always thought I could handle the road, but then I went right out and wrecked my vehicles because, lo and behold, I could not. This time was no exception, as I went off the road and felt my convertible rolling sideways rather than forward. Those new tires and I rolled over three times before we came to a stop—on the roof. Add one totaled Datsun to the tally. Do not feel bad if you are sensing the need for a calculator at this point.

Ron with his totaled Datsun

The first police officer who arrived at the scene found the car on top of me. Thinking I was already dead, he searched the area to see if anybody else had been thrown from it. Upon coming back to the car, he noticed me pulling myself out from underneath it! This "cat," it seemed, had a few more lives in him. When you consider this was a car with nothing but a flimsy windshield frame to prevent me from being crushed, I could not call it luck. Someone was just not willing to let me die at my own hands.

After giving my life to Christ, I looked back on this event, and others like it, and I knew it was one of many miracles God had accomplished for me before I ever knew Him. This was the third time I should have been killed. I was taken to the hospital in Hugo, where I stayed for a week before my brother came down from Aurora and took me to the Colorado University Hospital. It was while I was there that I finally started understanding what was happening around me. To this day, I have no personal memory of this accident. I had suffered a traumatic brain injury but no broken bones.

When I got out of the hospital, I knew I needed to get a better job to start paying the bills, which drastically increased from everything connected to my accident. I reapplied to the highway department, became a flagman, and worked nights at a service station to make ends meet. However, that was not the only activity I engaged in to generate income. Having still failed to learn much from life, I purchased a pound of marijuana, thinking it would be pretty easy to sell, and I needed the extra cash.

One afternoon, a young boy came to the door and asked if he could purchase some of my stash. He was a friend of a friend, so I thought it would be safe to sell him some. My mistake. Who knew he was the county commissioner's son who had agreed to go undercover to keep his own rear end out of jail? I told him we needed to set up a location to meet, somewhere other than where I was staying (give me some credit), which ended up being a spot along the new interstate highway being built. We got together, made the exchange, and I went home happy with some marked bills in my pocket.

Heading back to town, I got pulled over by a police officer who immediately arrested me for dealing. Not only did his search find the marked bills, but the officer also discovered a small quantity of speed in my pocket. When they searched the house where I was staying, they also found the rest of the pot. Fortunately, the speed never made it to the police report. Still, I was arrested and taken to the county jail in Hugo for the pot. So much for my plan to change my life, as I found myself sinking once more into the whirlpool of bad behavior, drugs, and alcohol.

With everything that had happened to me in the previous six months, I had no money to hire an attorney. I was assigned a court-appointed counsel who did some investigating and found out that the county commissioner and the prosecuting attorney had set me up. My bail was set for $50,000, which I did not have. The alternative was to pay a bondsman $5,000, which I borrowed from my brother Roy Lee to purchase my freedom. The charges were dropped later under threat of an illegal entrapment charge against the commissioner and the police department.

When I got out of jail, I learned that the family I had been staying with had decided to move to Loveland, so on top of my other problems, I was homeless once more. I still had the job at the gas station but had been fired by the highway department. A U-Haul franchise operated out of the station where I worked nights, so I spent several months storing my belongings in unrented trucks or trailers. A friend of Rose's family was the cook and the maintenance person at the Limon Country Club, and he let me use his apartment there at the club to take showers and even to do some laundry. To summarize my life at the time, if you are having trouble keeping up: I was a broke ex-con living in a gas station, hanging with my ex-girlfriend's brother, storing my stuff in rental trucks, showering and doing my clothes at a country club, eating fast food at a local diner, and "living the dream."

God Begins a Work

Things began to look up a bit when I landed a decent job working for the Kyburz Construction Company, building a local nursing home. I finally saved up enough money to rent a small trailer house close to Limon High School. Not long after I started at Kyburz, I discovered some of my new friends lived in Dillon, which was the gateway to many of Colorado's finest ski areas.

In the meantime, Rose and Kenny, who had converted from Catholicism to a Protestant denomination, had come to believe God wants a personal relationship with us, even royal screwups like me. Fortunately, they were still involved in my life and still cared for me, joining the chorus of voices telling me that I needed to turn a corner before I ended up in prison or as roadkill on a highway somewhere. This could have been due to me getting so drunk at a poker game in my boss's trailer that I could not even remember how I got home. The next morning, when I woke up and found my motorcycle parked outside my door, I called my boss to ask what had happened. He told me that I was so drunk I could not hold the bike up to get it started, and it fell over on me! My friends came out of the trailer, picked us both up, got it started for me, and then held it up while I got on and somehow drove the ten blocks to my trailer. What was that about friends not letting friends drive drunk? Looking back on it later, I knew it was just another way this Jesus, that I wanted nothing to do with at the time, had surrounded me with His angels, knowing what He had in store for me, and it was not this.

Kenny and Rose started quoting the Scriptures to me during our times together, and that was the first meaningful time anyone shared the love of God with me. Before long, the Bible started coming to life, as I had never experienced in church as a kid. I was at least willing to listen, and it actually began to make some sense. As a result, in March of 1975, I "prayed the prayer" with my friends and was baptized in the freezing cold waters of the Limon Airport Pond. Looking back on it, I had to admit this was somewhat like those infant baptisms where we do not really understand what we are doing, or perhaps we are doing it more to please others than due to any sort of authentic desire. Yes, at the time I thought it was a genuine experience, and there were some changes my fledgling faith made in my life, but they paled in comparison to what occurred when I later made an authentic conversion.

Shortly after my baptism, a lady named Jenelle, with a pickup truck loaded down with furniture and personal belongings, came in wanting to rent one of our U-Haul trailers. She was headed to Texas to meet up with a man she had met on an internet dating service. I thought she was quite attractive and a really nice person to talk to. We hit it off right away while I was getting the trailer ready, sharing personal things you do not normally talk about with customers over a countertop. However, soon she was off to Texas, and I figured I would never see her again.

Regardless of the authenticity of my conversion, positive things started happening around me for a change. After Jenelle returned from Texas, her hoped-for relationship having failed to materialize, she inquired in Limon about me and was told I was at Saint Luke's Hospital recovering from the mugging incident that had occurred just one month after I was baptized. She made the near-hundred-mile trip to my bedside to see how I was doing! When I was released, Jenelle drove me back to Limon to get my stuff and move it to Denver. "Someone above," it seemed, arranged for an apartment for me in Denver through the mother of my hospital roommate!

My ophthalmologist informed me that I needed a career change and that remaining in any physically demanding work, or sports activities, could seriously and permanently destroy what little eyesight I had left. I could not afford another blow of any kind to my head. He told me to take it easy for a while to give my eye a chance to heal. During that time, I had ample opportunity to reflect—again—upon my life: what had gotten me to this state of affairs and how I might take advantage of recent good happenings. God has a lot to say about accountability, and though I was not a committed believer by any stretch of the imagination, the need for far more of that was constantly on my mind. It had become abundantly apparent that most of my wounds were self-inflicted, and a change of scenery was not the solution. I needed to focus on changing me.

The good fortune in my circumstances continued as the assistant manager at the new apartments where I was living took a liking to me and was a big help. She was an older woman who sometimes seemed overly concerned with my situation—doing my grocery shopping and helping me navigate my new surroundings. Due to my blindness, it was hard to get around the apartment building and its facilities by myself. Anywhere there were stairs, gates, unforeseen obstacles, or narrow passageways posed a real problem for me.

Most seeing people do not realize just how difficult it is to get around on the most straightforward paths in life, like finding a place to sit down to relax or eat. Without adequate sight, the moment you step out of the familiarity of your room, the world can become a terrifying place. This is why so many blind people become hopelessly homebound. They get tired of the fight, the fear, and the chaos of doing simple things everyone else takes for granted, so they will only go where they feel safe.

However, as time went on, the sight in my right eye improved to where I could get around pretty well on my own. When the assistant manager moved to another apartment building several miles away, I figured that I could help people like she had done, so I applied for and was hired on as the new assistant manager there. In a short time, I discovered that watching her and doing the job were two different things. Apart from the fact that the position seemed to make me attractive to the women in the complex, I decided it was not for me. A college degree, with a resolve to learn something this time, was the way to go. I enrolled at Metro State College to complete my degree in business with a minor in accounting, with the intention of becoming a CPA.

When my eyesight recovered enough for me to drive again, I returned to Limon to get my motorcycle from a friend who had kept it for me. It came in handy, getting me to and from jobs and back and forth to the college. I was not driving legally at that time because during the day I could not tell if the stoplights were red or green, other than by watching the cars in front of me ... as if I had not learned anything from all my previous accidents on my bike. Brilliance, it turned out, is not gifted. It is learned.

A New Relationship

After Jenelle helped me move from Limon back to the Denver area, she left, and I never saw her again. Oh well, angels come and go. I began dating an older lady I met in the apartment complex who had been a model during her younger days. Her name was Penny, and she lived with her teenage son and daughter. Later, the landlords decided they did not want to lose me and were nice enough to remodel a one-bedroom and a two-bedroom into one large three-bedroom to accommodate us when, surprise, Penny and I moved in together.

One day, when I came home early from classes at Metro State in 1976, I went into the apartment Penny and I had moved into and discovered her daughter having sex with a young man. When I told him to hit the road, it made her very upset, and from that point on, she began devising ways to get even with me. She was only fourteen then, so I felt I could not keep this a secret from her mom. When Penny found out, she was furious and grounded her, which only strengthened the daughter's resolve to get revenge.

This, combined with the other trials of being a single mom to two teenagers, led Penny to drink a lot. She started a relationship with a new friend, Jack Daniels, and hung out with him in front of the TV from the time she came home from work each evening until she went to bed. The task of making dinner for everyone and keeping the apartment up soon fell on me.

Later that fall, Penny's daughter and a friend came up with a plan to exact her revenge. While I had quit the assistant manager position, I was still working part-time doing minor maintenance on the units. These two girls started spreading rumors that I was having an affair with a young lady living in the apartment building who had started helping me paint vacated apartments. Rumors like that spread like wildfire, especially in a closed environment like an apartment complex where most people knew me due to my job.

Of course, the rumors got back to Penny, and we talked about it one night over dinner. When I started questioning her daughter about it, the teen picked up her dinner plate and looked like she was going to throw it at me. I rose from the table in self-defense and pushed her away, while at the same time seeing Penny's fist heading toward my face. As I saw what was coming, I had a flashback to the mugging that had nearly caused me to go blind, and my need to protect my eyes at all costs took over. I threw one arm up to block her thrust, and with the other, I pushed her away forcefully. She tripped over the coffee table and fell backward, resulting in some bruises and, you guessed it, another visit from the boys in blue.

I guess blood is thicker than love as Penny took her daughter's side when telling the cops what had happened. I was arrested on a domestic violence charge and taken back to a place I had hoped to never see again. I went before a judge and was told I needed to take some anger management classes before I went to court. Psychological counseling and more anger management training were recommended at the hearing. With a domestic violence charge on my record, I could not stay with Penny, and without our combined incomes, she could no longer afford the large three-bedroom apartment we had occupied. She had to move back to her mother's house, and I moved into a one-bedroom in the complex. Pretty much done with Penny, her daughter, and all the drama, over the next nine months or so I dated a few other women, but none of them seemed to want a serious relationship like I did.

Totally Blind!

This brings me back to the incident that opened the book and the time a few years after the mugging, where the road eventually ended in total blindness. I had been holding on to hope for three years that my eyesight, now hanging by a thread after that fateful night, would not get any worse. However, in early February of 1978, I started seeing floaters in my right eye, and I knew this spelled trouble. All my past trips to eye doctors told me it was a good indication that I was experiencing another retinal detachment. A couple of weeks later, I went under the knife to have scar tissue removed from around my failing right eye, and yet another laser treatment to reattach the loose retina. Apart from some faint light perception, I came out of that surgery totally blinded. It took me back to those moments sitting on the curb outside that bar crying, "I'm blind. I can't see!" It was not a time I ever wanted to relive, but here I was.

My mindset was that things would never get better. Without sight, I lost my job at the apartment complex. Now officially unemployable, I had to apply for supplemental security income, a government subsidy for people with qualifying disabilities like mine. With my world officially turned upside down, I had to decide what I would do with an existence now cloaked in darkness. Do I continue to pursue a degree in business? Do I still want to be a CPA? Seriously, who would hire a blind accountant? I could almost see the ads for my new firm: "I know I cannot see your numbers, but I am really good with math!"

I enrolled in a Colorado state rehabilitation program to get evaluated concerning what my next steps might be, understand new mobility techniques, and start to learn how to read Braille. During that time, my mother came down from Washington to try to convince me to move back to Colville, and my oldest brother, Leslie, came down from his new residence in Missouri with the same message. They both wanted me to return home so Mama could take care of her baby boy for the rest of his life. Bad idea, I thought. First, I did not believe Mom would outlive me; and second, I never in my life of eye troubles wanted anyone to feel sorry for me or to baby me. All I ever wanted was to be treated as a normal person, but lacking that, I certainly did not want anyone's pity. I had to decide on my own what I would do with the rest of my life, and it did not include running to Mama's house with my tail between my legs.

Moving On and Moving In

After many tests and evaluations, I learned at the rehab center that I had a very analytical mind and that perhaps the best possibility for me was to get a degree in computer science. I had already taken some classes along those lines and was intrigued by the field. When I changed my degree from accounting to computer science, everybody thought I had lost my mind and that I would never be able to write computer software without my sight. I did not want people's pity any more than I wanted them telling me what I could and could not do. In fact, that only stiffened my resolve to, like Frank Sinatra's famous song goes, do it "my way."

Speaking of music, in the fall of 1978, while still at the apartment complex, a guy across the hall befriended me, and he and a couple of his friends taught me how to play the guitar. It was encouraging to know I could make beautiful music (well, I thought it was beautiful anyway) by feeling the neck and the strings without seeing what I was doing. Moments like this gave me hope that I could do new things well, even without my sight.

Later that fall, some friends from my old apartment complex and I moved into a three-bedroom rental in Englewood. It was much larger than any home I had lived in up to that point, with a huge backyard and a spacious entertainment room downstairs where we set up our stereo system. One of my new housemates introduced me to a fellow Metro State student named Nancy. She had an apartment down on Capitol Hill closer to the college. We soon started dating, and then, true to form, I more or less moved in with her during the week, coming home on weekends when I did not need to be close to the school.

When would I get the memo that moving in with someone soon after you meet them simply does not work? If someone will do that with you, won't they do it with someone else? Such was the case with Nancy. I found out the entire time we were together she was also sleeping with one of her professors at Metro. She thought this arrangement was okay and did not want things between us to change, but call me old-fashioned, it did not fit well with my plans or the way my parents brought me up.

My next adventure with the opposite sex came in October of the following year when an RTD bus I was waiting on in the snow and cold unexpectedly passed right by my stop. Terrific, I thought, a blind guy standing all alone in the snow and the local transportation service ignores him. As I was yelling in the direction of the bus, a woman pulled into a service station behind me to fill up and recognized me as someone she had seen at Metro. She came over, introduced herself to me, and asked if I needed a ride. Her name was Mickey, and as we drove to the college, she also offered to drive me home that afternoon.

During our commutes, we talked and learned a little bit about each other. I hated all the time and trouble taking the buses cost me, so I offered to buy her gas and pay for her parking space at the college if we could make this a regular gig. She jumped on that because, being a student, money was tight for her. Shortly after that night, we decided to start dating under one condition: I had to be able to find her house on my own. She did not know at the time how efficient a blind man could be at such things, but she agreed.

Shortly after that arrangement started, we (sigh) decided it might be a good idea for us to combine our assets and live together. After a couple of months, I started feeling guilty over the whole living-together thing and thought we should get married. I had lived with too many women with far too little success, and it had never led to even one long-term relationship, much less marriage. I decided it was different with Mickey, and I loved her enough to take the plunge. Though she was not as certain about it as I was, she relented, and we set a date in May, the week following graduation.

My graduation on May 12, 1980, was a snowy, dreary day. Still, I was truly honored to be awarded "The Least Handicapped Person" on the Auraria campus where Metro State was located. I received a standing ovation as I walked across the stage to get my diploma, which my mom, who had come down from Washington, was able to witness. The following week (one week before the wedding) I was surprised when family from Washington to Missouri to California all showed up in force for the event. It turned out Mickey already knew, and everyone had decided to surprise me. Many of my professors also showed up for the wedding, and one of them even served as my best man. I did not want to have to choose from among my brothers, so this seemed the best way to go.

It turned out God had other plans for my wedding night, as that was the very night the spectacular eruption of Mount St. Helens occurred less than 400 miles as the crow flies from my home in Colville. Naturally, everyone cut their plans short and scattered to their various homes the next morning. A few who had flown in got stranded for nearly a week as many flights got canceled due to the spreading ash clouds after half of the mountain was blown sky-high by the devastating eruption. Some of the lethal vog (volcanic smog) made it all the way to Colorado. I finally get a woman to say yes, and this happens on our wedding day. It seems the "for better or worse" thing was going to get tested early.

Over the next few months, with a college diploma in hand, I focused my time and energy on job fairs, filling out resumes, and going on interviews that would kick off my career in computer science. Inasmuch as I knew it would not be easy to get an initial job as a blind programmer, I was willing to go anywhere, except I did not want to work for oil companies or the government. I took the first job the State of Colorado Department of Labor and Unemployment offered me, rewriting all the technical manuals into layman's language so their employees could actually understand them. Such resolve in such a young man, you must be thinking.

Struck Again!

It seemed my old friends "injury" and "near-death experience" were never far away, no matter how hard I tried turning over new leaves in life. During an evening in early December 1980, I was on the way home from work, and as I was crossing a street with the "Walk" light, a ten-ton city bus making a turn hit me and knocked me out! I was given an asphalt facial as I slid down the street on my face for approximately twenty feet. Can't a guy catch a break now and then and land on his butt or something? Anywhere but the head, face, and eyes!

I was rushed to the hospital in an ambulance, and when I regained consciousness, I found a nurse digging the asphalt out from around those eyes that had suffered such abuse all my life. She asked me those same questions NFL players get on the sidelines after getting their bells rung: what is your name, where do you live, and are you married? Obviously, the "how many fingers am I holding up" question did not apply. After feeling for my wedding ring, I remembered I was married but could not recall my address or phone number. Once I was admitted to my room, they would not let me sleep due to concerns that I had a severe concussion. The authorities later told me the impact of my head on the window of the bus cracked it from top to bottom. Poor window—should have known better than to take on this noggin!

Adding being hit by a city bus to my already impressive, or should I say infamous, list of accidents that might have killed me, this "cat" was still racking up those nine lives. However, two days later, I was back at work. Unfortunately, this latest impact had cost me my very last bit of light perception, which was all I had. It is a truly frightening thing to be cast into utter darkness permanently. It is sort of like being in a dark, scary cave when your only flashlight goes out.

Well, that was life before Christ. There are many more stories I could talk about—the endless partying, girlfriends, and stupid choices I made—but you get the point. However, as a favorite Easter message at church goes: "That was Friday. Sunday is a comin'!" My life, who I was, and all I thought was important was in for a big change.

Chapter II:

FAMILY AND FRIENDS

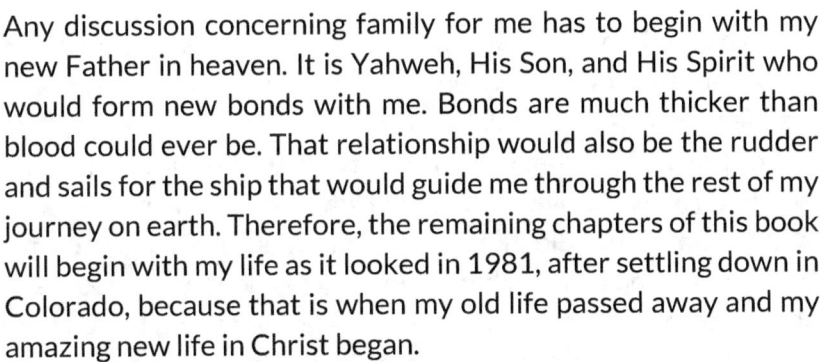

Any discussion concerning family for me has to begin with my new Father in heaven. It is Yahweh, His Son, and His Spirit who would form new bonds with me. Bonds are much thicker than blood could ever be. That relationship would also be the rudder and sails for the ship that would guide me through the rest of my journey on earth. Therefore, the remaining chapters of this book will begin with my life as it looked in 1981, after settling down in Colorado, because that is when my old life passed away and my amazing new life in Christ began.

Though my future seemed to be moving forward that year, my past was still my past, and my drug abuse problems arose once again to haunt me. In March, I was on my way to do a drug deal, but God was watching and had other plans. While I was waiting for the bus to take me to my score, a car pulled up and a couple offered to give me a ride. Funny how an adult using a white cane, indicating you are blind, has such an opposite effect upon people as Coke-bottle glasses does when you are a kid. Most people are very nice, and some offer unsolicited help, like this couple.

They were on their way to a piano bar, so I felt they would be safe to ride with. To my utter amazement, they started telling me about what God had done for me in sending Christ to atone for my sins and how much He loved me. Here I am, upset with God for allowing me to get hit by a bus, which resulted in me losing what little sight I had left. I am on my way to get drugs to medicate my pain away, and in the middle of it all, He sends me these two. I told them, "Yeah, I know all about God. I have been baptized." Nevertheless, I could tell they were not buying it. I gave the guy my phone number at work when he asked me if he could stay in touch, and he kept calling me. Soon, I found myself out to lunch with him, going to the museum and many other places where he continued to share the gospel and his testimony with me.

He explained how he had been busted for running a house of prostitution in downtown Denver and how he had finally admitted his life was out of control. He ended up asking God to keep him out of prison. He promised if the Lord would do that for him, he would turn his life over and serve Him forever. The man's name was Bill Fay. Little did I know, this man was a budding, soon-to-be-famous evangelist! When I told Mickey about our encounters, she reacted almost violently and did not want anything to do with Jesus. She did not even want Bill to have our home phone number.

But I kept meeting with him, like Nicodemus seeking out Jesus, knowing he had something I desperately needed, although I did not know what it was. Soon after that, he invited a pastor friend of his, named Jack McArdle, to have lunch with us. One of the first things he asked me was if I were to die tomorrow, did I have a clue where I would end up? I, of course, said no, but if he knew the answer to that question, I would sure like to know. After he finished explaining to me how God had sent His Son down from heaven to suffer and then pay the ultimate price on the cross for me, and that if I would just accept His gift and follow Him, life would radically change, something just clicked.

I have heard people talk about "the Hound of Heaven" God sends into our lives to prepare us to meet Jesus. Well, this was my moment to surrender my life to Him. I thought of Rose and Kenny and how they had played a big part in preparing me for this hour. Before lunch was over that day, I prayed with Bill and Jack, opening my heart to the One who promised to forgive me, love me, and guide my life from that day forward. I sensed the Holy Spirit entering my body and my soul, and everything changed. Whatever was going on inside me at that moment was decidedly not me. Some incredible force—a loving and merciful yet powerful force—was assuming control at my deepest gut level, totally transforming how I would come to see and feel about everything from then on.

I had always been the stubborn individualist who never let anyone control his life; but I sensed that Jesus was truly good, was not an enemy I needed to defend against, and He wanted only what was best for me, so I turned my life over to Him! It would no longer be the crazy kid from the country "blindly" bouncing off the walls in life. It was like I was seeing the world through new eyes, and it felt amazing!

I quickly let Mickey know about this amazing new journey I had begun, and I started attending Pastor Jack's church. Shortly afterward, Bill invited us to his house for dinner, where he challenged Mickey to consider what Jesus had done for her and to make the same decision I had. Bill was no stranger to this evangelism thing and knew it would not go well for either of us to be, as the Apostle Paul described, "unequally yoked." He asked her to pray and ask God to show her a sign to prove that He existed and loved her.

The very next day, as she was driving to school, she heard Bill's voice in her head, repeating his request for her to pray. So, Mickey prayed and asked God to show her a sign. The next weekend, she and I went to a concert at Boettcher's Concert Hall downtown, and when we returned home, I realized my wallet was missing. I had to go to the neighbor's house to call the venue to ask them to look for my wallet because the phone company was changing our home number and had canceled our old service. No luck, but they said they would contact me if anything turned up.

To add insult to injury, Mickey made some crack about my wallet being gone forever, and the only way it would ever return is if some "goody-two-shoes Christian" found it. Things looked bleak, and it seemed like this situation was helping to prove her point. Then, two days later Pastor Jack came knocking at our door and handed my wallet to Mickey! When Mickey asked him where he got it, he told her she needed to call Bill Fay. When she did, Bill told her that on Sunday morning, there was a ladies' Bible study at the concert hall, and one of the ladies found the wallet in my seat! When she went through the wallet, all she could find was Bill's business card. She contacted Bill, and the wallet was turned over to him. Bill, in turn, delivered the wallet to Pastor Jack. God had answered her challenge! Not only had one of those "goody-two-shoes Christians" found it, but the wallet had passed through the hands of three people to get back to me!

In 1984, with Mickey still floundering in her decision for Christ, she found a coupon that allowed us to spend a week in the Cayman Islands. We made reservations to fly there and to stay in a condo we found on an Airbnb site. We participated in several different activities during the week and took tours around the island. One of the places raised turtles for commercial use, so when I saw turtle steak offered at a local restaurant, it turned me off. However, once I tried it, I found it to be quite good! Anyway, at the turtle farm, there was a post office called hell. You cannot make this stuff up, folks. So, I picked up a postcard and sent it to

Pastor Jack. On the card, I wrote, "Pastor Jack, you told me that if I did not change my ways, I would end up in hell. Well, here I am!"

One of the days, we went out on a catamaran with some divers who submerged with their spear guns to catch various goodies to bring up and serve later as our meal on a small island nearby. This reminded me of the story of Jesus after His resurrection, when He made breakfast for the disciples on the shore, and Peter jumped out of the boat due to his excitement at seeing his risen Lord. That was what I visualized the day we were on the beach eating the fish the swimmers had caught and prepared for us. It was a great vacation for Mickey and me, there in the light and warmth of the sun, but it could not hide the dark clouds that were beginning to gather on the fringes of our relationship that were not solely from her side. I was becoming increasingly uncomfortable with the idea of being married to an unbeliever (2 Cor. 6). I knew I could never go back to my previous lifestyle; neither did I want to spend my life with someone whom I could not share my love for Jesus with.

Later that year, Mickey came to Alta with me one weekend to watch a skiing competition I was participating in, as well as to get in some skiing herself. Unfortunately, a guide I was to use for the race decided to be cute and try to get me to ski as close to Mickey as he could before he had me stop. I ran into Mickey and knocked her down, which reacquainted me with my old friend, temper, and Mickey had to hold me back from knocking the guy down! This physical incident did nothing to bring us together spiritually, and I must admit it was not my best witness for Christ in her eyes.

Divorce on the Horizon

In 1986, some good things and some not-so-good things happened between me and Mickey. On the positive side, she decided to join the Kairos Prison Ministry I was involved in at the women's prison in Cañon City. Mickey then decided to join an Episcopal church closer to home than the one we had been attending in Denver. On the other hand, while at that church, she decided that she wanted to become an Episcopal priest. I wondered how someone who did not want to give their life to Jesus could still want to be a priest. I also had a tough time dealing with this because I was not sure if I approved of their doctrine or of women leading men. It seemed the Apostle Paul had much to say about the places of men and women in the church, and I did not see changing cultural movements as a reason to violate those scriptural truths. This only led to further marital problems between us. I was trying to do everything I could to save our marriage, but the Titanic had sprung too many leaks.

The year 1987 started out with a bang, literally, when Mickey and I went to Los Angeles so I could take some training for my Air Force programming job. Mickey came along with me so she could go to Disneyland while I was at the conferences during the daytime. Our evenings were basically free time. It promised to be a lot of fun, combined with a little work, but it ended up being something entirely different as the Whittier earthquake struck the area! What was it that made the world blow up every time I had something special planned?

The marriage continued to deteriorate, and just to do something special, I decided to take Mickey up to Redstone Castle. I was hoping we could reopen some lines of communication and share feelings we both knew needed to be brought into the light. I loved Mickey and did not want our marriage to continue down the path it was currently on. But it seemed that no matter how hard I tried, the darkness continued to overshadow our relationship.

Later that summer, I found out Mickey had bought a fur coat without my knowing it. When I questioned her about this, along with some other things that she was doing without my knowledge, the rift between us became a chasm. When I engaged a friend to look over a few receipts, we found that every time Mickey went to the grocery store, she charged an extra forty dollars in cash on the credit card. At that time, we were trying to reduce our debt, and so I questioned her about it. Her response was that our marriage was not working, and she wanted a divorce. This was the last thing I ever wanted, but I knew neither of us was happy with the status quo; so I asked her what she wanted from me, and she told me she wanted her share of the down payment for our townhouse. After some negotiations over other items, we finally agreed upon a settlement.

During the spring of 1989, my marriage hanging by a thread, I decided to go a few days early to a beep baseball board meeting. Beep baseball is a unique way for vision-impaired people to play baseball. (This is discussed further in chapter IV.) I flew to Springfield, Missouri, where my oldest brother was living at the time. He owned and managed a chain of convenience stores there, as well as in Kansas, Arkansas, and eastern Texas. One thing he and I had always had in common was that we were both entrepreneurs and really enjoyed the business world.

The first night at his house I was hoping to break into a conversation about the Lord by simply blessing the meal, but it all fell flat when he informed me this was his house and prayer was not on the agenda. You can say just a few words to some people, and they are eager to meet Jesus. With others, you can talk until you are blue in the face, and they want nothing to do with Him. The Bible says we can plant seeds and water them, but only the Lord provides the growth; as an evangelist, I can tell you this is true. We do not save anyone, for only God can provide the conviction of the Holy Spirit.

Upon returning to Denver from a fishing trip later that year, I walked into an empty house because Mickey had used the occasion to vacate the premises and my life. She took everything, including most of the furniture, so I had to go shopping the next day to refurnish the home. The furniture I could replace, but Gordy, my guide dog, was also gone. I tracked Mickey down to get Gordy back and make one last, futile attempt to try to talk her into going to counseling. She refused to consider it. I must admit to mixed feelings about this. Again, I felt that as a Christian, I should fight as hard as possible for my marriage; but it takes both partners working together to reconcile a marriage.

Early in 1991, still licking my wounds from the divorce, I learned a female friend I had met at church was going through a divorce. It seemed there was no saving her relationship with her husband any more than there was the one Mickey and I once enjoyed, so we started dating. We were hesitant to talk about marriage, having both recently emerged from failed ones. To trust your feelings for a person at such times would be both foolish and naïve.

Soon after, she told me she wanted to date other men just to get a handle on what direction her future love life should take. What with all the previous relationships I had been in that bombed, I was not overly optimistic about tying myself down to one person, either. Heck, I did not have a clue where that part of my life was headed, so I decided to do what the Bible said to do in uncertain times: fast and pray. I was pleasantly surprised a few months later when God actually honored my fast and answered my prayers. It would not be with this woman—no, He had someone else in mind.

My Miracle Girl

God has led me into so many incredible circumstances due to my visual problems. In March of 1991, He introduced me to a very special young lady, named Shannell, when I was in Houston for the spring board meeting of the National Beep Baseball Association. I came to call her my "miracle girl," not just because of the phenomenal talents she possessed, but because I found out her mother had been told by doctors that she would never bear children.

I arrived on a Friday night and was in the lobby of the hotel with Lassen, my new guide dog, when this thirteen-year-old girl noticed us and wanted to meet him (Ah! Lassen, the chick magnet). She approached and wanted to know all about him and why it seemed there were so many visually impaired men there that evening, which led to a discussion concerning beep baseball. When I asked what she was doing there, she said she was there for the Stars Across Texas Competition, and she invited me to come and watch her. Of all the visually impaired men there and with all the dogs, why did she pick me? She had no idea I was a music fan and a musician myself. Some would call this a coincidence, but I call it a God-ordained divine appointment.

Later that evening, I took her up on her invitation and went and hung out in the back of the ballroom to hear her and many other supremely gifted young people perform. As it turned out, I was totally underdressed in my T-shirt and jeans, standing there among people wearing tuxedos and suits, but nobody seemed to mind. I discovered that Shannell was not there to compete but to sing the song she had won the competition with the previous year. What a voice! After her performance, Shannell led me over to talk to her parents. We had a wonderful discussion, and then she asked them to help us do a photo op, with Shannell, Lassen, and me.

Before leaving, Shannell invited me to come and hear her perform at a bar the next evening. Of course I went and stood next to what I thought was one of the speakers because the music and her voice were so clear. When she finished, and I commented about how clear and lifelike the music coming from the speaker was, she laughed and said, "No, silly. The reason it sounded like I was right next to you is because I was standing about a foot from you, singing my songs to you as though you were the only one in the room!"

Would all this have happened to me if I were just one more man standing in a crowded hotel lobby on a Friday night? I do not think so. Anyway, after the night was over, Shannell's parents took me back to the hotel, and we talked some more. Though I cannot see it, I still have and cherish the copy of the photo she sent to me with Lassen, herself, and me. I have had it described to me in detail. We eventually lost touch, and I do not know what happened to her or her career, but for a couple of incredibly special nights, she meant the world to me.

Finally, God's Choice for Me

That summer, Lassen was looking quite shabby, so I took him to a groomer. When I went to pick him up later that day, I missed the bus we needed to get home. Missing buses was a regular occurrence for me; so we began walking to the next stop, where I knew I could catch another one. However, after waiting for that bus a while, I surmised I must have missed it as well. Inasmuch as that bus only ran once an hour on weekends, I decided to hitchhike home.

Lassen was strutting his stuff, with his beautifully groomed coat and a blue bow on top of his head, when a lady drove by. She noticed Lassen and me, but having been warned by her dad to never pick up a hitchhiker, she continued on her way. However, within a couple of blocks, the Lord seemed to say to her in an inaudible voice, "Turn around. The man is not going to hurt you, and he needs your help."

After introductions, Yvonne gave me permission to put Lassen in her car. Lassen took over the back seat, and I sat on the passenger side of the front seat. She noticed I was wearing a cross, and we started talking about the singles group at her church. I told her I was interested in joining a singles group, which led to her writing her phone number on her business card and giving it to me.

The following week, I was in Topeka playing in our first beep baseball tournament of the year. After returning home, I wanted to go out for a ride on my tandem and thought of the lady I had met two weeks earlier when I was hitchhiking. So, I went down to my neighbor's house and had them read the phone number on her business card (we blind folks do have our ways). She was at my door fifteen minutes later, ready to give piloting my tandem a try. Seems we had at least one thing in common: we were both pretty fearless and always ready to try something new.

We had not ridden far before discovering she was too short to reach the hand brakes on my large-frame tandem. We made it back to my townhouse and ran the bike into the garage door to stop it. It was such a beautiful day, we decided to walk through my neighborhood. We had been walking for over an hour, when we realized we were lost. We could have been in Kansas for all we knew. Nonetheless, Yvonne was very impressed when I directed us to a main thoroughfare by just listening to the traffic patterns on the streets. I had honed that skill by then, having had to walk or ride or take RTD everywhere.

That three-hour excursion gave us lots of time to talk and get to know each other, which led us to start dating. I found out she had three daughters: two of them were living with her, and the third one was living with her father in Castle Rock, a few miles away. I also found out she lived less than a mile from my townhouse, so getting together would be easy. Both of her daughters warmed right up to me and Lassen, the chick magnet. Then, the Lord brought my mind back to my fasting/prayer retreat, and I smiled.

At the time, Yvonne had a fair commute across town working for a company called Protex, which manufactured additives and cures for concrete. Yvonne's boss had become a good friend with whom she fellowshipped at Cherry Hills Community Church. I was working just a few miles south of her work at Lowry Air Force Base. It was not too far out of her way to drop me off, so we started carpooling together. It also became a routine for us to alternate dinners at our separate homes. She would cook for me at her house, then the next night I would cook for her at mine. Many times, we had Yvonne's boss join us, or the boss would invite us over to her house for dinner.

Over time it became obvious to both of us marriage was in our future, but I knew before that happened, she would need to meet the family back in Colville. In July, we flew up there, and everyone immediately fell in love with her. It was clear they all thought, as I did, that Yvonne was the real deal. From that point on, we started making serious wedding plans, knowing how we felt about each other and that we now had the family's blessings. Despite their blessing on our relationship, none of them made the trip from Washington to Colorado to attend our wedding. I suppose I understand, this being my second marriage. Family and friends are all-in for your first marriage, full of hope and good wishes. But a second or third one? Now it is about wondering if you will get it right this time, so wedding parties can be somewhat smaller.

Given this, we decided our celebration would be small. Yvonne's mom and stepdad came in from California, and we invited a few of our close friends. Once again, Yvonne's boss stepped in and offered her home for the event. We were married on August 23, 1991, only ten weeks after we shared our first date on my tandem bike. We went to Ouray, Colorado, for our honeymoon, enjoying the natural settings by day and a few nights hanging out in the hot tubs.

One of the ways I came to know Yvonne was the real deal, the one God had chosen for me, was by the way she took immediately to all the crazy sporting events I had become involved in over the years. She actually trained to be a guide for me when I went skiing. One of the few places we did not find harmony, however, was our church preferences. I liked the smaller-sized congregation that leaned Pentecostal, and she preferred a local mega-church with Presbyterian underpinnings. As important as God was to each of us individually, and to our marriage, we decided this would not do and that we needed to find a church where we could both feel comfortable. After trying several different ones for a month or so, we finally found one that was a church plant from Cherry Hills Community Church but was smaller and had a pastor whose message moved both of us. That is where we decided to put down roots.

In late July of 1992, my oldest brother, Leslie, who lived in Missouri, was flying home to Washington (with a layover in Denver) for his thirtieth high school class reunion. We picked him up at the airport in Denver and brought him to see our home and to enjoy some of my homemade chocolate-raspberry ice cream with us. This was another divine appointment because it was the only time Yvonne would get to meet Leslie, and the last time I would ever see him.

The following May of 1993, my voicemail carried a message from my sister that Leslie had passed away from a massive heart attack. He was only forty-eight years old.

I immediately arranged to fly home to Washington to help with funeral arrangements for the first of the Barton clan to pass from this life. While this was a tragedy for sure, it helped me understand how fortunate I was that I did not have to worry about physical death in this life, for God has an eternal place prepared for me in heaven.

Back to August of 1992 when Yvonne attended her first World Series of Beep Baseball, held in Saint Louis Park, Minnesota. On one of those evenings, as Yvonne and I were eating at a Perkins restaurant, a woman I had dated years before recognized me and came to our table. She was the daughter of a Baptist minister who had tried unsuccessfully to convert me back then. Some plant, some water, and some harvest, as the Bible says, and I am sure she took pleasure in knowing she had influenced my life for God. To my complete surprise, we found out she was married and living just down the street from us. Unfortunately, before we could build on that relationship, she passed away from cancer, but I think God wanted her to know that her efforts to plant seeds in me had borne fruit.

Special Times Back Home

In the summer of 1993, a month or so after Leslie's funeral service, Yvonne and I flew back up to Washington for a surprise fiftieth wedding anniversary party for my parents. They never had a wedding reception, so the family had planned to make up for that by rolling out the red carpet for two people who meant so much to so many over the years. When Yvonne and I arrived in Colville, we were whisked off to the home of one of my brothers so as not to spoil the surprise. We spent days secretly cleaning and decorating the old Grange Hall because it had not been used in years, but my parents had many fond memories of events there when they were young.

On the special day, family and friends secretly gathered at Douglas Falls Park, one mile from my parents farm. My youngest brother used my dad's tractor to pull the hay wagon, which he loaded with several bails of hay to sit on (a limousine, country-style). A few cousins, grandchildren, and Yvonne and I sat on top of the hay for a ride back to my parents' farm. My brother pulled the wagon up close to my parents house to pick up mom and dad for a ride back to the park where our surprise celebration would officially begin (this was the first time they knew we were in town).

A fond memory for me is the custom T-shirts that my sister designed for everyone to wear. All the shirts had gold stars, "The Barton Allstars," and "50th Anniversary" printed on the front. The back of each shirt was tailored to who wore it. My dad's shirt said "Coach," my mother's said "Manager," the shirts for my siblings and I said "Major League" along with a "number" that correlated to our birth order. Our spouses shirts said "Expansion League," and all the grandchildren's shirts said "Minor League." When my parents first laid eyes on everyone, the word "surprised" would not suffice to describe their response. It was more like "shocked." After a barbeque at the park, we all moved to the Grange Hall to continue the long-overdue celebration (including a dinner, dance, and wedding cake) for a wonderful couple.

In the summer of the following year, Yvonne and I attended a church retreat at Camp Trail West in Buena Vista, and I quickly became friends with a young lady and her parents when we went on an early morning horseback trail ride. As I mentioned before, I am thankful for the opportunities my lack of sight affords me to form rapid relationships with complete strangers. At the end of the trail, there was a campfire set up where the staff cooked eggs, sausage, and pancakes over a fire. The cook made a game of tossing the pancakes back over his head to each guest standing in a line twelve feet away; and if we wanted pancakes that day, we had to catch them. Knowing of my blindness, this aforementioned young lady came up to me and asked me if I wanted her to catch those pancakes for me, and I gladly accepted her offer.

People are so much nicer and less intimidated when they know that you need help and they can be the ones to give it. There is no clash of egos or fear they might have in talking to a stranger. Having a disability puts you in a subservient position to others that removes any perceived threat. This is a particular blessing in my prison work (discussed in chapter III), where my blindness immediately removes any macho competition concerning power or position. Power is a cherished commodity behind prison bars—those who have it abuse it, and those who do not typically are abused. However, with me it has never been a problem because the guys do not see me as a threat.

In May of 1996, I got a call from my dad asking me to come home to Washington to go fishing with him on Memorial Day weekend. This was the first time Dad had ever called or invited me to do anything. Though he did not specifically confess his spiritual conversion, it was obvious to me that he had become one of God's children. Gone was the temper that had always characterized him, even when our boat got caught on a big boulder in the Columbia River. That sort of thing would have unleashed a tirade of epic proportions in the dad I had known.

One of God's greatest gifts to us is reflected in Jesus' words to His disciples after being resurrected, "Peace be unto you." The Holy Spirit truly puts a peace inside of us that the world cannot give, because it comes from God. My father, the man I had been witnessing to for years, had become a living example of God's peace. Looking back, I know God put this trip together. It was no coincidence, for it would be the last time I would see my dad alive. I believe God wanted me to know my dad had found redemption before he passed away.

Saying Goodbye to Dad

When we returned home from a camping trip in California, where I got to meet Yvonne's dad, Will, I received the sad news that my father had passed away from a heart attack, just like my oldest brother, Leslie. Dad had always said he wanted to die with his boots on, and that is exactly what happened. Mom and Dad had gone into town to pick up his tractor from the repair shop. Mom typically followed him back home, but she made a stop at the store. When he did not show up at home, she went out looking for him. She first spotted his tractor across a large field. It took a while to find him because the tractor had traveled a significant distance before running into a tree. Dad had fallen off the tractor shortly after it went off the road and was likely dead before he hit the ground.

I was able to play and sing a couple of songs at my dad's funeral, hoping to inspire those attending to consider who God is. Given my ministry today, I get more than a few opportunities to oversee funerals. I always make it a point to remind people that none of us has a guarantee that we will see tomorrow. So, whether they are unbelievers who need to know Him or believers who are not engaged in following Him, I encourage them to seek the Lord. Where we end up spending all our tomorrows will be dictated by decisions we make today, and none compares with a decision to fully embrace Jesus Christ.

Another hurdle I had to face that year was the breakneck pace I was keeping in my life, which was starting to wear on Yvonne. She was tired of spending so much time alone. One problem was the time spent at the retreats, as well as the time spent preparing for them. So, I reduced the retreats to two per year and stopped serving at the Territorial Correctional Facility in Cañon City, focusing solely on Fremont Correctional Facility.

Fast forward to May of 2003 when Yvonne and I took our mothers on an Alaskan cruise with Princess Cruise Lines out of Vancouver, Canada—something my mom had never experienced. She was a very picky eater, who did not eat much at all. Having raised nine children, she was always more concerned that her kids had enough to eat, even if she had to go without. The two moms shared a cabin and became good friends.

Needless to say, meals on the ship could not have been further from what we grew up with, and Mom was blown away! No one had ever waited on her like they did on that cruise ship, and I had never seen her eat that much. She must have put on ten pounds that week. It was the biggest gift I ever gave Mom, and I am so glad we got to share this memorable experience together. None of us suspected how little time we had left with Mom.

Two years later, my sister in Washington called to report that Mom had passed away. At the memorial service for Mom, I just could not pass up the opportunity to remind everyone of the choice they need to make as to where they want to spend eternity. I also got the opportunity to perform my mother's favorite song, "One Day at a Time."

Despite the loss of both of our parents, the Barton family is still a strong and close-knit group, due largely to my parents' influence. So, around the middle of July 2011, we scheduled a Barton family reunion out at one of our aunt's homes in Colville. Yvonne and I decided to drive so we could take my guide dog, Lizzie, with us, which meant more people doting over my dog, more questions about my blindness, and more opportunities to witness for Jesus. After spending a few days in Colville at the reunion, we drove to Tacoma to visit my uncle and aunt on my mother's side of the family. They were believers in Christ, and it was a great visit. They are now in heaven with Him.

Good Times Along the Coast

We then continued our trip through Oregon to go tuna fishing with the Parkins (who raised and socialized Lizzie). Lizzie was able to reconnect with her great friend of the four-footed variety. Another dog, you may ask? Well, not actually. As soon as Lizzie got out of the car, she ran straight to the fence and went nose-to-nose with the donkey! It was hard to tell who was more excited, Lizzie or the donkey! This was the first time Yvonne was able to witness the unusual bond between the two, and it brought her to tears.

The tuna we caught fishing off the Parkins' boat averaged around thirty-two pounds, and what made it enjoyable to me was how hard the fish fought. Once we had caught a total of twenty-five, we pulled in our lines and headed back to the mainland, stopping to check our crab traps on the way. It seemed our lucky day, for we netted sixteen to twenty crabs along with our haul of tuna. As we arrived back at the dock, more friends and family greeted us with a crab-cooker and a grill for the tuna. Yvonne and I thought we might have died and gone to fisherman's heaven that evening. It was not just the experience of the fishing trip, but the love we felt from the Parkins, who did all this for us out of the goodness of their hearts.

The next morning, we headed down the coast of Oregon into California to visit Yvonne's dad in Modesto. As we headed toward Oakland to visit Yvonne's cousin and his wife, we stopped to tour the local vineyards. When we arrived in Oakland, they took us to dinner at the Moose Club, where the blind guy had more opportunities to share his faith. Then it was on to Yvonne's father's home in Modesto. We attended church with him, met his pastor, and I was invited to share my testimony with the members of the congregation. This was one of the many times I heard the words, "You need to write a book!"

Fast-forward again to 2014 when Jerry, a good friend and ministry partner, invited a couple of us from the ministry to join him for three days at their family fishing derby in Buena Vista, Colorado. It began Friday afternoon, and all fish had to be weighed by noon on Sunday to qualify. We started at Antero Lake with little success, so we decided to try a different spot on Saturday. Ditto the lack of success. It was beginning to look like the event was going to be a bust for us.

Then on Sunday morning, we stood in the parking lot of a local tackle shop and prayed, asking the Holy Spirit to give us guidance as to where we might have the best luck for our final morning. Jesus was pretty good at locating prime fishing spots during His life here on earth, so why not ask Him where to lower our nets? Having learned to trust my relationship with Jesus, Jerry asked me what I was hearing. My response was that I thought we needed to go to Twin Lakes. Sometimes you hear God audibly, and sometimes it is just a hunch you feel in your gut; but when you learn to trust God, you honestly believe He will answer you, even with such simple requests as this.

Once we got Jerry's boat launched onto the lake, we headed out into fairly shallow water not too far from the shore. We had been fishing for an hour and a half before a fish finally took my bait. Then I wondered if it might just be a snag, because it did not seem to move. As I was telling Jerry I thought my line was hung up, "the snag" started to move out toward the middle of the lake. I was not pulling on it; it was actually pulling the boat! I was just hoping this would not be the "big one that got away" story. Jerry had not anticipated catching such a large fish, and he had given me a ten-dollar Walmart Special rod and reel with an eight-pound test line! I had to act and react very carefully as the fish and I dueled for around thirty minutes, with me letting up and then gently pulling in, so as not to break the line. The fish finally tired, and my friends were able to get it into a net.

RB and his winning catch

It was getting close to the time our catches had to be logged, so even though others wanted to continue to fish, we had to get back to camp. When she hit the scales, my baby logged in at 20 pounds and 34 ½ inches. This fish was more than enough to win the derby, so I got the grand prize and bragging rights for at least one year. When people marveled at my catch, I joked, "You should have seen the one that got away!" Unless somebody else catches another monster lake trout, that record will continue to stand because I trusted in my Heavenly Fishing Guide.

Under the Knife

After retiring from the federal government in 2010, I started concentrating a little more on some physical issues I had been dealing with for several years. One of the issues was my right arm, which had become hard for me to lift, much less carry any weight. I went to an orthopedic surgeon and found I had a torn rotator cuff that required surgery. When I had the procedure done in June of that year, it proved to be the most painful surgery I ever experienced and one of the longest to recover from. Over the years, I have endured more than my share of surgeries, in addition to the many I had done on my eyes when young:

- In May of 2015, I had my left hip replaced, and then in September, my left shoulder went under the knife. With all the injuries I had sustained to that shoulder, I received one more lifetime achievement award of a different sort in the form of debilitating arthritis that made it hard to sleep at night, much less function during the day. I was once again reminded that shoulder surgery was far more painful, and the recovery time far longer than it was with knees and hips.

- In January of 2018, I had a knee replaced that was out of alignment. It amazed me that just a few short hours after the surgery, a physical therapist came and gave me a walker and sent me to walk the hallways. The therapist was tethered to me, and it was not long before she was saying what so many other coaches in various pursuits had: "Slow down! I cannot keep up with you!" After arriving home, I discovered far too many obstacles to navigate around the house, so Yvonne would take me to the local recreation center, where I would walk one to two miles around the track every time we went. My total recovery time took less than eight weeks. "No hill too big for this climber and God," I thought.

- In January of 2019, my other knee went under the knife. I checked into Porter Hospital at 5:30 a.m., and right after lunch, the physical therapist came and took me out with my walker once more. Once again, my total recovery took less time than anticipated, which was just another example of how God had taken care of me over the years and how fast He brought about healing from my many surgeries.

- In January of 2021, it was time to have my other hip replaced (if anyone's counting, that makes a clean sweep of hips, knees, and shoulders). Does anyone remember the TV show *The Six Million Dollar Man*? To this day, they have to wand me whenever I go through metal detectors at airports or the prison because of all the metal in me.

Surprise!

I love springing surprises on people, and in 2016, I pulled off a whopper for Yvonne's seventieth birthday. Hey, I figured this would be no problem for a guy who had organized national sports tournaments and numerous ministry retreats over the years, but organizing events where everyone knows what is going on is one thing. Trying to keep Yvonne in the dark until the "big day" took my organizing skills to a whole new level. Between sons, daughters, sons-in-law, daughters-in-law, grandkids, and friends of the family, dozens of people were going to be involved. Not only did I need to figure out how to keep it all under wraps until it was time to spring the surprise on her, but I had to figure out how to lure her away from the house so we could get everything set up on the patio for the party. We used some members of the family, whom Yvonne already knew were in town, to get her to run an errand with them. When they returned to the house, the shock and awe Yvonne displayed reassured us that all the traps we had sprung worked. She did not have a clue, and the rest of the evening turned out to be something truly special.

It turned out I was not the only member of my family who loved to surprise people. In August of 2017, my nephew Matt threw a surprise birthday/anniversary party for my older sister and brother-in-law in Lake Tahoe. It would be one of those "go big or go home" events that moved beyond surprise to shock and awe. This one was rather unique in that my older sister and her husband were born on the same day and then got married the day before they shared their twentieth birthdays. So, this celebration would mark both their fiftieth wedding anniversary and their seventieth birthdays. Like I said before, you cannot make up this stuff.

The highlight of this trip was a day at a ropes course strung through the redwoods. You think you have been on a high course? Not this high! It was a great opportunity for the blind guy to participate and share with the family how, no matter the challenge, we can always trust in God to protect and take care of us. There were three levels of difficulty, and everyone else went for the beginning level. Not me. I like "flying blind." Although my blindness was not my choice, it is now part of my "walking by faith, not by sight" blessing. I could not see how high I was, so there was nothing to fear.

I had learned through the thousands of miles on my bike, alpine skiing, and all the times this "cat-with-nine-lives" had survived when I should have been seriously injured or killed that God is watching over me. It did not take long before just about everyone else decided to follow me to the advanced course, especially when they noticed a sizable crowd gathered to watch the crazy blind man hanging out in the tops of the redwood trees.

As the holidays approached in 2018, we invited Yvonne's oldest daughter, Annette, and our son-in-law, Dave, to come over for Thanksgiving dinner. While we were enjoying the feast, Dave started talking about a new electric smoker he had bought, sharing the different meats he was now able to prepare. One of his favorites was bison burgers. I knew right away that I had to get one of these "babies." You know, the whole food and me thing? I love any opportunity to expand my repertoire of great recipes and to add to my already scrumptious menu of custom ice creams. Now, I could begin experimenting with providing equally tasty meat dishes. My new smoker enabled me to cook ribs, briskets, and prime rib roasts so tender you can cut the meat with a fork or pull it off the bone with your fingers.

The World Shuts Down

As 2020 arrived, the surreal phenomenon of Covid-19 cast its shadow over the earth, and it seemed to stop spinning. Many of my pursuits you will read about in later chapters, which dominated my attention, came to a standstill; and for a go-getter like me, that was really hard. Nevertheless, not being one to give up on life, I found other ways to fill my time. Thank God for audiobooks! I listened to more books—more than I had "read" in all my years up to that time. I proceeded from one to the next to the next, and I checked out the complete *Left Behind* series by Jerry Jenkins. Yvonne and I had read through that series twenty years earlier, but I enjoyed it even more the second time around.

Fortunately, flight services were not shut down for too long, and Yvonne and I were able to fly to Florida to visit her daughter, Amy, our son-in-law, James, and our two granddaughters; and to see the new home they had purchased a year earlier. While we were there, I got an opportunity to check out Amy's stationary bike. It was similar to the ones we used at my local recreation center. I enjoyed it so much that we decided to buy our own stationary spinning bike when we got home. To this day, at age seventy-five, I still ride our bike at least three times a week.

With my own bike, I can ride anytime in the morning I want to, without worrying about how to get to the recreation center or how crowded it might be there. I do not have to wear a face mask, and I can listen to my music programs, which act like a metronome to help pace me. I ride to the beat and actually enjoy myself! This has led me to an even better workout than at the rec center because I enjoy the whole experience so much more. Nonetheless, I do go back to the rec center from time to time to socialize with the friends I have made.

Fast-forward to Christmas of 2022, when we got the sad news that my older brother Roy Lee had passed away. Due to his stubborn attitude of refusing medical help because "no one knew his body like he did," we never found out the reason for his death. We just heard he was very weak and had trouble breathing toward the end, so we are not sure if it was pneumonia, Covid-19, or something else. Unfortunately, I had not seen Roy Lee in over three years, and it is painful for me not to have had an opportunity to talk to him about the Lord when his health was failing, and now to not know where he is spending eternity. It would be wonderful if everyone we know and love was going to spend eternity in heaven, but the truth is all we can do is point them to God and pray they make the right choice.

On the Fourth of July weekend, 2023, I flew to Spokane, where my brother-in-law picked me up at the airport and drove me to Colville to attend a belated memorial service for Roy Lee. I hoped I would get the opportunity to share the good news of the gospel with both family and friends during the service, but that was not to be. Instead, I had to try to speak to them individually. You could say I was a man on a mission, reaching out to those closest to me in this life. Everything God has done for me, including my loss of physical sight, is for the express purpose of giving Him honor and glory.

Chapter III:

BROTHERS IN GREEN

In the fall of 1982, my life changed in a pivotal way. Bill Fay asked me to be a volunteer on the very first Kairos retreat at the Fremont Correctional Facility in Cañon City, Colorado. The Kairos ministry got its name from the Greek word for time—a special time that is set aside for God. After volunteering at that retreat, I realized God had been molding me my whole life for this. It became the match that struck the candle, which lit the way to my life's work and joy. This chapter contains the truths God has been teaching me for more than forty years that have shaped my thoughts and character. They are what have made me, "me." My greatest hope for you in reading my story is that you will either give your life to Christ or develop a deeper walk with Him. As I look back at all the things I have gone through over the years, I see how God was preparing me for prison ministry. God has redeemed my drinking, the using and dealing of drugs, the number of times I was in and out of jail, and the addiction to pornography by using these experiences as a way to relate to what the inmates have gone through. I can look back now and know it was only because of the grace of God that I am even alive to be able to share His love with others. I have come to resonate with the Apostle Paul's words concerning why Jesus was tempted: "Because he himself suffered when He was tempted, He is able to help those who are being tempted" (Heb. 2:18). No lemons exist that God cannot turn into lemonade. Every seemingly bad thing that has ever happened to us can be redeemed and used for good in the lives of others around us, if we will just let Him use us. Jesus said, "For everyone who asks receives, and he who seeks finds, and to him who knocks it will be opened" (Matt. 7:7–8). I hurt for my brothers and sisters who have never discovered God's purpose for their lives, because I know how exciting and fulfilling it is when you do.

The Community Steps Up

This ministry could not exist without a team of dedicated volunteers on both the outside and the inside of those prison walls. We bring into the prison all of the snacks and meals that act as incentives for the inmates to sign up for the reunions and the retreats. On the three-day retreats, we provide incredible meals for lunch and dinner on Friday and Saturday, with lunch on Sunday—the kind of food the inmates will not get from their mess hall. They say the way to a man's heart is through his stomach, and nowhere is that truer than with men used to prison food.

But it is all good, for once we get them there by feeding their bodies, we can do what we really came for, which is to feed their souls with the good news of God's love for them. We also have the "inside" team, made up of inmates who have previously benefited from the ministry and are mature men of God. They have the responsibility of serving us while we are there, along with attending to the day-to-day needs of their fellow brothers in green in our absence. Together with God, we make a pretty formidable team!

My major task on the Kairos retreats has been worship leader, and I love it. There is a reason virtually every church service begins with music. Music prepares us for the message God wants us to hear. Music penetrates our defenses, reaches into our inner man, and is a powerful tool for directing our thoughts and emotions. Therefore, it can be used for either good or evil, and we see the effects of this throughout society today. It is a privilege to bring good, uplifting music, used in the cause of infusing truth to these men, who for the most part have spent their lives listening to music employed in the cause of darkness and deception.

As I was getting involved in Kairos, I convinced a good friend of mine named Joe to become a volunteer along with me. Joe was a black man (he is now with our Lord), but we were as close as blood brothers. One of the ladies on our blind bowling league could never get our names straight and was always calling me Joe and him RB, so we made a joke of it and began to refer to ourselves as identical twin brothers. When I introduced Joe to the rest of the prison ministry team, we decided to refer to ourselves as "identical twins," and that handle spread to the inmates at the weekend retreats. Inasmuch as 50 percent or more of the inmates participating are either black or Hispanic, this was a great ice breaker.

Perhaps for the first time in my life I felt grounded—secure in both who I was and the people in my life. I was happy and fulfilled: no more aching doubts concerning who I was supposed to be or what I was supposed to be doing. I no longer felt the need to drink myself into a stupor in an effort to medicate my pain. God was in my life, He was "working all things together for my good" as He promised, and His Spirit had become the only medication necessary.

Introducing Kairos to Limon Correctional Facility

In the fall of 2002, we began organizing what would be our first Kairos retreat to be held at the Limon Correctional Facility (LCF) in October. It was then I felt the Lord calling me to leave my position in Cañon City and start volunteering exclusively at LCF. It was in Limon I was mugged, and my journey of "walking by faith, not by sight" had begun, so it seemed fitting that the journey had come full circle. One of our first priorities was to put together our inside team because our outside team was pretty well established.

One of those inmates, a man named Michael Chambers, had been on my very first Kairos weekend in Fremont in 1982. He and I had become close friends there, but I had lost track of him and did not know that he had been transferred to Limon until we both worked that very first LCF retreat. Michael was a huge, intimidating black man whose appearance others told me was frightening, but inside he was as gentle as a teddy bear. He and I becoming friends was one of those times when my blindness broke down walls because I could not see how he appeared; I only heard what was in his heart. Michael became part of our inside team, as well as part of our prison worship team. He had a deep baritone voice and was also a member of the LCF choir.

It was on that retreat weekend that I was asked if I would consider leading the Kairos retreat in 2003. Over the previous twenty years, I had been asked many times to do this, but this time the Holy Spirit prompted me to accept. I had always enjoyed, and felt it my calling, to just sit at the tables and share with the guys who were our focus. But when I felt the Holy Spirit nudging me to move, I surrendered to take on that role.

God's timing is always perfect, and this retreat was no exception. Several close friends, including one I had lost touch with who had served with me in other facilities, were there at the closing. I was able to recruit them to help me with the retreat, and one of them stayed on with me as an assistant for many years after that. I love it when God's plan is so clearly revealed!

I remember well Captain Butch, who was the Director of the Faith and Citizenship Volunteer Programs (all programs brought into the prison from outside sources). He was your typical gloom-and-doom military sergeant type, constantly telling us we were wasting our time at LCF and that there was no way we were going to change the men he had come to know. The only response we could give him was that he was absolutely right: we could not change anyone at that sort of deep level, but we served a God who could! God is the author of transformation, and He is ready, willing, and able to do that very thing!

As it turned out, two inmates who were brothers attended that retreat: Dave was an inmate on our inside team, and his brother Joe was a participant on the retreat. They had a profound effect on ol' Butch. You see, these two brothers hated each other and knowing this, Butch was hesitant to let Joe participate. But God worked a miracle on these two brothers over the weekend, to the point where they were standing arm in arm at the end. I do not know if it made a believer in Christ out of Butch, but it sure made him a believer in the ministry! Yes, I believe like Dr. Seuss's Grinch who stole Christmas, I actually saw the captain's heart grow a few sizes after that weekend.

Over the years I have seen God work miracles as several prisoners—hardened by family dysfunction, social isolation, abuse, general chaos, and criminal lifestyles—surrendered their lives to Jesus Christ. Only God, through the indwelling of His Spirit, can transform us from the inside out into something brand new. God makes the changes. Some take time, and some happen instantly, but all are miraculous! He can give us joy, hope, and peace that the world cannot give, whether we are on a battlefield, in a homeless shelter, or in a place as depressing and hopeless as a prison cell.

I realized how precious God's timing was on that weekend. Of all the other retreat weekends I could have answered the calling to lead, it was the third Kairos retreat at LCF where I really felt the Holy Spirit convincing me to accept that role. I will never know if the same outcome would have taken place if someone else would have been leading that retreat besides me; but in either case, I was truly blessed by witnessing the impact on Captain Butch and those two brothers. Besides the very first Kairos retreat at Fremont, this became my most memorable retreat at LCF.

It really is amazing to come month after month, as we do for our half-day reunions, and see the authentic joy in these men's hearts (many of whom are shackled with life sentences with no chance of parole) as they worship and fellowship with us. Jesus calls us to love Him with our whole heart and to love others as ourselves. Our brothers in green participate in a genuine Christian community because of the critical element of time spent together and the restrictions placed on them that don't allow them to pursue selfish goals and objectives.

Kairos to Ekklesia

What began under the Kairos banner at the Limon Correctional Facility suddenly needed to change. Once again God revealed His humorous side, showing me that what goes around comes around. LCF is a Level IV state prison. Certain things the Kairos rules require us to do cannot be done at LCF. So, after discussions broke down over the contrasting demands of Kairos and the prison, the Kairos Colorado Council informed the Department of Corrections that the Kairos ministry could no longer operate there.

However, the warden at that time contacted Dick Evans, who was the coordinator for our group, and said this concerned him because our ministry had done such excellent work and had such a positive influence on the men at LCF. He did not want us leaving over something like this; so he suggested we change our ministry name. Thus, we all voted to become the Ekklesia Prison Ministry.

We go into the prison once a month for what we call our half-day reunions, and the three-day retreat weekends are held twice a year in the spring and the fall. Because of the space restrictions of the facility, we have around thirty of our brothers in green attend the reunions, but we are limited to twenty-four on the retreats. There is a lot of preparation in advance of the weekends in the form of training sessions for the volunteers, soliciting donations for the food we provide, getting the food list to the warden for approval, preparing music and messages, and so on.

The three-day retreats are great opportunities for volunteers and the inmates to get to know one another, because the same two to three volunteers will stay with the same six prisoners for table talks the entire weekend. These relationships continue through the full-day reunion the following Saturday.

The goal at the reunions is to get to know new inmates and disciple those who have previously made decisions for the Lord as to what a relationship with the Lord should look like. Since we focus on building relationships, it is crucial that our volunteers are committed to this ministry if they want to be involved at all.

Ekklesia operates under the following mission statement: "To build relationships and restore lives to Jesus Christ through the witness and testimonies of volunteers gathered together, and all in accordance with the essentials of faith and a relationship with Jesus Christ." The vision statement is "to give hope and healing to those who are incarcerated at the Limon Correctional Facility through sharing God's love, mercy, grace, and forgiveness."

It was in the prisons where I first learned it is *all*—EVERYTHING IN EVERY WAY—about Christ working in me through His Holy Spirit to glorify God! People ask how I have become who I am. This opens up opportunities to point them to Christ, not me. In comparison, any time I spend working on my own goals or aggrandizement is wasted time.

A good friend named Jerry, whom I had led with at Kairos, became our very first leader for Ekklesia when we changed the name in 2012. All in all, the first retreat went very well as God reminded us that this was not our ministry, but rather His ministry, and we are there to serve the men who are incarcerated at LCF. We are to love those men and let them know God is calling them by name and offering them His gift of forgiveness.

It is important to note that every team has an important role. As God describes the church body, where each part is important, the same is true with the prison ministry, where each team member has a vital role to fill.

Jesus said it was for our benefit that He leave; for if He did not, the Holy Spirit would not come. Jesus told His disciples, "I have much more to say to you, more than you can now bear. But when he, the Spirit of truth, comes, he will guide you into all the truth. He will not speak on his own; he will speak only what he hears, and he will tell you what is yet to come" (John 16:12–13).

Therefore, I pray and listen to what the Holy Spirit is telling me to speak about, instead of trusting my own thoughts, when I am speaking to my brothers in green.

God wants the Spirit to guide each one of the team members to be the leaders He has called us to be. We believe the inmates that participate on the three-day retreats are there because God invited them. So, the Spirit always connects us to those inmates He wants us to minister to. Likewise, the Spirit specifically calls the team members He wants to work a three-day retreat. As I learn to put my trust in God to guide each one of the volunteers, I also trust Him about which volunteers will be present. He knows who will be there, what they need to hear, and how to use each one of us if we simply remain obedient, humble, and attentive to His Spirit.

The Messages of Ekklesia: Choices

Our Ekklesia manual includes many different outlines the ministry deems important to touching the inmates "where they are." While we are encouraged to use these outlines, we must also seek the Lord's guidance as to how to personalize them. One of the first talks I give is on "Choices." Given that our brothers in green have made more than a few bad choices in their lives, this is a topic that needs to be covered on every retreat. I am no stranger to bad choices, and it is an effective way for me to relate to them and them to me. The loss of my sight, and what God has done through it, is the best tool on my belt.

I let them know we all make bad choices. For some, it may be easy to make bad choices, but it is harder to deal with the consequences because of the lack of any family support. I was blessed growing up with both of my parents. However, a great number of the inmates I have known over the years have not only come from single-parent homes, but they have also suffered all manners of abuse: verbal, physical, and mental. It makes me genuinely appreciate my parents; for in spite of all my dumb choices, I always had their love and support to fall back on. Our brothers in green did not have the guidance or direction to make correct choices, nor did they have a safe harbor to retreat to when they got into trouble. It is no wonder to me that so many of them wind up incarcerated. I tell them they now have a new family, the body of Christ, to fall back on and a Father who will never abandon them.

In closing, I let them know, while God will never abandon us, He allows us to choose between His way or our way. We determine our course by our conscious choices. Then I ask them to remember the reasons and the results of those choices, and how important it is to make the right ones.

Over the years, a number of folks that I have shared my testimony with have asked what my thoughts are on being able to lose their salvation. So on a personal note, I share how I have struggled with the same question: whether I can forfeit my salvation after I accepted Jesus Christ into my life. I am comfortable acknowledging that I do not fully understand this subject. What I do know is that the Scriptures are very clear that the greatest sin I can commit is denying Jesus Christ. When Jesus prayed to the Father in the garden (John 17), He clearly stated that He had not lost one that the Father had given Him. With everything I have been through in my life, it is clear to me that I am His child, and I know He will never forsake me. As I see it, the bottom line is whether a person has truly accepted Jesus into their life in the first place. Romans 10: 9-10 states, "If you declare with your mouth, 'Jesus is Lord,' and believe in your heart that God raised him from the dead, you will be saved. For it is with your heart that you believe and are justified, and it is with your mouth that you profess your faith and are saved."

God's gift to us is the saving work of Jesus Christ on the cross. He poured out His blood to pay the penalty for our sins. The Bible is very clear that we are saved by grace and not by works, but it also states that faith without works is dead (James 2:14-26). For me, just knowing how much God loves me inspires me to share my story with as many as I can.

Action

This is the one talk that fits me the best for sharing with my brothers in green. I always kick it off by singing the song, "Why Me" by Kris Kristofferson, where he asks the Lord what he has done to deserve His favor, what he has done to deserve God's love, and how he can perhaps pass on his experience to lead others to God. I was a prideful, stubborn troublemaker with a huge chip on my shoulder most of my life until Jesus Christ showed up and turned my life upside down. Ever since then, all I have wanted to do is show others what I went through before I met Jesus. This topic is similar to talks I have given on what it means to be a Christian: inasmuch as providing a physical witness of my faith means actions others see in accordance with believing in God.

To help describe those actions, I use the analogy of a three-legged stool. It is critical we share our faith, both through evangelism and discipleship, for "faith comes from hearing, and hearing by the word of God" (Rom. 10:17). The first leg is opening the door by asking Jesus into your heart, but that only "opens the door." John said those who received Jesus were "given the *right* to *become* children of God" (John 1:12, emphasis added). The Gospels speak of the many people who said they wanted to follow Jesus while He was with them, but few truly did. When He told them that following Him would not be easy, many turned back.

The second leg is personal discipleship, which comes through consistent times of prayer, studying God's Word, and fellowship with other believers. A favorite verse of mine concerning my growth process is found in James 2:26, "As the body without the spirit is dead, so faith without works is dead." God has called me to share my story as a witness of God's love for each of us. That is what Christian action is, loving one another. In John 13:34–35, Jesus said to the apostles, "I am giving you a new commandment, that you love one another; just as I have loved you, that you also love one another. By this all *people* will know that you are My disciples: if you have love for one another."

The first two legs are for the individual, and the third leg, which is "action," will draw all three together. In my case, that is where God has called me, as one of His followers, to share my story with everyone. So, in order for me to bear fruit, I need to be engaged in fellowship, to share my story, and also let others know that God loves them and that He is inviting them into His kingdom. This also includes praying, spending time in His Word, fellowshipping with others of our faith, spreading the good news of His coming, and serving the needy, without which I cannot honestly call myself a disciple of God.

I always embrace the triple A's of my faith: *Accepting* God's grace by opening my heart to Jesus Christ and asking Him in; *acknowledging* that I am a follower of Jesus Christ by boldly sharing my testimony with anyone that will give me the opportunity; *acting* on my faith by trusting in the Lord to always protect me, and also doing what the Holy Spirit is calling me to do. No matter what trials I might be going through, I always give thanks to God, for it is through our trials and tribulations that we are strengthened. It is my hope that my brothers in green will follow my example and become more intentional about sharing Christ with their fellow inmates. I let them know they might be the only Bible their friends will ever read.

When Jesus stood before a group of Jews who wanted to stone Him, He asked them for which of His many good works they were judging Him. They said they were not condemning Him for His good deeds but for His words that they considered to be blasphemous. It is difficult for people to condemn good deeds they see you do; and when your words come in conjunction with those good deeds, it is hard for them to ignore or dismiss them. This is why all three legs of the stool must be present and functioning for our witness to be effective.

In the Bible, God asks the question, "Whom shall I send?" (Isaiah 6:8). Will we step up when God sends that "wee, small voice" of His Spirit to call us to action? A favorite saying in the world of sports is "the greatest ability is availability." It does not matter how gifted a football or basketball player is if he is constantly injured and unavailable. Peter says we "have been given everything pertaining to life and godliness" (2 Pet. 1:3), but boldness is a decision. Will we step up when God sends that "wee, small voice" of His Spirit to call us to action? Anyone reading this book who is a believer knows the feeling of receiving a prompting and failing to act, including me, and the regret you feel afterward.

Jesus will never force Himself upon anyone. Many times, in the Gospels, we read of Jesus' *compassion* being the reason He ministered to people. So, compassion for people without the boldness to intervene in their lives for God gets us nowhere. Likewise, boldness without compassion means we are doing it for all the wrong reasons.

When people ask me if I am a Christian, I ask them to define what a Christian is; then, based on their answer, I let them know if I am a Christian. I am surprised how many different versions I hear from people when I ask that question, when the answer is simple and uncomplicated. My definition includes those three legs of the stool and how that leads to relationships with God and others.

In giving my testimony, I always include a little about how I lost my eyesight and how God turned, what many consider to be a tragedy, into a blessing. I relate to the story of Joseph in the Old Testament—how his brothers sold him into slavery and how what they meant for evil, God used for good. The men who took my eyesight did not know they were unleashing God's power for good in my life!

Rock-Solid Friendship

In 1992 I was introduced to a gentleman by the name of Bo Mitchell. He had recently been released from federal prison where he served a one-year sentence for doing something he had no idea was even illegal. He had borrowed some money to help a couple of friends start a church, which the law calls a straw loan.

Straw loans involve an "agent" obtaining a loan for someone who cannot obtain it on their own or for their intended purpose. Even though Bo had paid back the loan, the judge wanted to make an example of him. But being a man of God, Bo accepted this as something the Lord wanted him to experience, to wake him up from his fast-paced business life that left little time for his family and Jesus. Having spent so much time myself in prison ministries, Bo and I became friends very quickly.

One of my favorite stories of King David is in 2 Samuel 16, where a man named Shimei is cursing David and throwing stones at him. One of David's "mighty men of war" asked David for permission to cut off the fool's head. I think many, if put in David's shoes that day, would have told his warrior to go for it. But not David. His answer was truly one of "a man after God's own heart" as he replied, "If he curses, and if the Lord has told him, 'Curse David', then who shall say, 'Why have you done so?'" Godly people look at life's situations and ask, "Lord, what do you want me to learn from this?" If God's goal was to wake Bo up and reestablish his relationships with his family, it was mission accomplished! Bo and his wife later wrote a book together about that experience, called *Grace Behind Bars.*

Bo and his partner, Bob Beltz, had a talk show on KOA radio called "You Get the Blessing." Bo invited me more than once to be a guest on their show, where I shared my testimony with their listeners. One of the greatest gifts that resulted from losing my sight is seeing people through the eyes of Jesus Christ.

The "Son Glasses"

I like to challenge the inmates to take concrete steps toward action in their faith and what that might look like. A favorite example of this in my life is my now-trademark "Son glasses" featured on the cover of this book.

I explain how in 2019 I went to Las Vegas on a Narrow Gate Men's Retreat, where my friendship with Bo Mitchell deepened. As Bo and I were sitting at a blackjack table, he observed how people responded differently to me than they do sighted people, so he came up with an idea to purchase over forty pairs of sunglasses and put two stickers on the lenses. On the right lens is the word *Son* and on the left lens is the word *glasses*. He told the men at Narrow Gate to put these glasses on their desk at work or on the mantel in their homes, as a reminder to look at others through the eyes of God's Son, Jesus Christ.

Bo noticed that I was wearing my glasses every time he saw me, so he commented to me that he did not intend for me to wear them every day. The glasses were simply intended to remind the men at Narrow Gate to look at people through the eyes of God's Son. I told him, "But, Bo, you do not realize what an evangelistic tool these 'Son glasses' are because people are always stopping me and asking me to explain what the stickers on my sunglasses mean." I told him I do not have to wait until someone asks me how long I have been blind, or how I lost my sight before I can share my testimony with them. The "Son glasses" create more curiosity than just asking me about my blindness. I am always looking for an opportunity to share my testimony with anyone I come in contact with. At our Narrow Gate Christmas party later that year Bo presented me with a much nicer pair of sunglasses with the same stickers. This is my example of how I am serving Jesus. I then ask the men, "What is yours?"

Forgiveness

Forgiveness is another three-legged stool: accepting *God's* forgiveness, forgiveness of *self*, and forgiveness of *others*. Then I share a little of my personal testimony about the unforgiveness I was hanging on to before I accepted Christ into my life. For many years, I was a heavy drinker and drug abuser, due in part to unforgiveness. I blamed my problems on all the people who harassed me and made fun of me because of my limited vision. There was that instance where, if I had I not passed out in a drunken stupor, I actually intended to shoot a police officer! I felt rejected and hopeless, and I lashed out at others like a cornered animal. I was not honest enough to accept responsibility for the things I had done, so I blamed others.

I remind the men of the most famous prayer in the Bible, the one called "The Lord's Prayer" (Matthew 6:14-15). Jesus states, "For if you forgive other people when they sin against you, your heavenly Father will also forgive you. But if you do not forgive others their sins, your Father will not forgive your sins." The importance of forgiveness is a major part of Jesus' life and teaching.

Peter once asked Jesus, "Lord, if my brother keeps on sinning against me, how many times do I have to forgive him? Seven times?" Jesus replied, "No, not seven times, but seventy times seven." Then Jesus tells a parable about a master who had forgiven the debt of a servant, only to find that the servant refused to forgive a debt that was owed to him. The consequences of this were severe. Jesus concludes by saying, "That is how my Father in heaven will treat every one of you unless you forgive those you need to forgive" (Matt. 18). Then I tell my brothers in green about the men who were responsible for taking my eyesight—how I hated them for a long time. But after I accepted Christ, I knew I had to forgive them. In the process of forgiving them, I realized how God had used this event to turn my life around. I tell the guys that I would probably be sitting with them, instead of standing in the front of the room ministering to them, if it was not for that.

I refer to Matthew 6 and one of those uncomfortable truths we do not like to consider: if we do not forgive others, then God will not forgive the wrongs we have done. Then I ask them if they believe God can change their hearts toward the people they are holding in unforgiveness—a tough question, especially when it comes to family, because so many of them have come from broken, dysfunctional homes. This reminds me how thankful I am to God for my parents. They loved me through thick and thin.

I tell them how God changed my heart concerning all the other people I held in unforgiveness from my youth. It is hard to believe forgiveness is possible, when our anger and hatred is so great; it seems nothing can help. I assure them, "With God all things are possible," and I am living proof of that. I go on to say, if I ever meet the men who mugged me and caused my blindness, I will tell them how God turned their evil act into something for good in my life. God has used my blindness to, literally, teach me how to "walk by faith, not by sight."

There is a powerful exercise we take the inmates through concerning forgiveness. We ask them to remember who they hold in unforgiveness. We pass out some water-soluble paper strips and ask them to write the names of those people they have trouble forgiving down on the strips. Those names could include family members, police officers who arrested them, prosecutors who badgered them, judges and jurors who convicted and sentenced them, jailers who wronged them, and other inmates who abused them. Some of them even need to forgive God for things that have happened to them. Then we hold a large jar of water at the front of the room and have them bring their slips of paper up and drop them in the jar—symbolically dissolving their hatred, anger, and unforgiveness in the living water of Jesus' love. This is always one of the most impactful moments of our weekends together, accompanied by a lot of tears and hugs among our brothers in green.

Lastly, unconfessed sin brings us under God's conviction. David painted a graphic picture of this in Psalm 32: "When I kept silent about my sin, my body wasted away ... for day and night Your hand was heavy upon me, and my vitality was drained away as with the fever heat of summer." Yet, David also provides the cure when he proclaims, "I acknowledged my sin to You and my iniquity I did not hide. I said, 'I will confess my transgressions to the Lord,' and You forgave the guilt of my sin." Under the New Covenant, James adds a new twist: "Therefore, confess your sins to *one another*, and pray for *one another* so that you may be healed" (James 5:16).

Without confession, there is conviction without healing. Say yes to confession and forgiveness, and healing will follow.

The Greek word for grace is *charis*, and its true meaning is the divine touch upon the heart and the evidence of that touch in your life. The two go hand in hand and cannot be separated. If there is no divine touch, which is the Holy Spirit who comes to indwell us when we invite Jesus into our lives, then there is no motivation or power for living a life of faith.

Self-Awareness

In order to get my brothers in green to think about how they feel about certain stimuli that might trigger their darker side—about what they like and what they do not like, about what is important to them, and more importantly, about who is important to them—I ask them to compare how they see themselves versus how God sees them. We are who God says we are! God has made it clear, if we have accepted Him as our Lord, we are a new creation (2 Cor. 5:17).

While I am on the subject of our identities, I share how I look at my identity. Up to the day I received Christ, I was a sinner. On the day I received Christ, I was a sinner saved by grace. Since that day, by the power of God's Spirit, I can say, "I am not what I used to be, and I am not what I am going to be!" My sin nature did not go away when I asked Jesus into my life since I still disobey Him by some of the choices I make, but according to Romans 6:6-7, I am no longer a slave to sin. I am completely dependent on the Holy Spirit to live according to His will. However, when we do stumble, 1 John 1:9 promises us, "If we confess our sins to Him, He is faithful and just to forgive us our sins and to cleanse us from all wickedness."

Who Is Jesus?

The purpose of this talk is to relay to our brothers in green evidence that Jesus Christ is who He said He is and how that uniquely qualified Him to pay the full penalty for our sins. I point out His humanity in that He worked, grew tired, and sat by a well to rest. He displayed righteous anger at the religious rulers who defiled the temple with their greed and taught religious rules and regulations, instead of God's truth. At the same time, Jesus loved to hang out with the common people like you and me, eat and celebrate a wedding with them, and play with their children. Another great illustration comes from the story of Lazarus' death and resurrection. Jesus wept over the death of His friend, revealing His humanity, but then raised Lazarus from the dead to show His deity. Lastly, we find Him weeping with great compassion over Jerusalem and setting His face like flint toward His ultimate goal.

Most importantly, Hebrews 4:15 states, "For we do not have a High Priest who is unable to empathize with our weaknesses, but we have One who has been tempted in every way, just as we are, yet He did not sin." Jesus was not spared any of the trials and temptations we endure as humans; in fact, he suffered more in the flesh than most of us will ever suffer. Jesus was indeed fully man and fully God. Philippians 2:6–8 says, "who, as He *already* existed in the form of God, did not consider equality with God something to be grasped, but emptied Himself *by* taking the form of a bond-servant *and* being born in the likeness of men. And being found in appearance as a man, He humbled Himself by becoming obedient to the point of death: death on a cross."

In the garden of Gethsemane the night before He was crucified, Jesus prays to His Father, "If You are willing, take this cup from Me; yet not My will, but Yours be done. ... And being in anguish,

He prayed more earnestly, and His sweat was like drops of blood falling to the ground" (Luke 22:42,44). Then He submitted to His Father's will, knowing that is what He came to do. In John 6:38 He says, "For I have come down from heaven to do the will of God who sent me, not to do My own will."

After Jesus' death, we find the apostles in great fear and trembling, thinking the temple leaders and Romans would come for them next. However, when the Holy Spirit indwells them, they are transformed. We find them preaching the good news of the gospel of Christ with boldness and power! His apostles saw Jesus taken up to heaven, and most of them died as martyrs rather than deny Him. If Jesus' resurrection was just a phony plot by the apostles, certainly, at least one of them would have confessed to avoid death.

Since that time, thousands of believers, who never saw Jesus in the flesh, testify that Jesus is their Lord, through the power of the Holy Spirit bearing witness to their spirits. He is indeed, "God with us" (Matthew 1:23). A final and most profound proof of His divinity lies in the millions whose lives have been forever changed by Him.

Three Encounters with Christ

The "encounters" in this talk are aimed at showing how Jesus dealt with different situations and how the brothers in green might relate to one or more of them. The first encounter is the story of the rich young ruler in Matthew 19:16–22. "A young man asked Jesus, 'What good thing must I do to get eternal life?' Jesus responded, 'If you want to enter life, keep the commandments.' The young man said, 'All these I have kept.' Jesus answered, 'If you want to be perfect, go, sell your possessions and give to the poor, and you will have treasure in heaven. Then come, follow me.' When the young man heard this, he went away sad, because he had great wealth."

The young man ran up against a fundamental truth of the Christian faith: if you want to hang on to Jesus, you have to grasp Him with both hands! To accomplish that, you have to let go of everything else, especially the temptations of the world. You cannot live with one foot planted in the world and another trying to find traction in the kingdom. It is like a trapeze artist who wants to switch from one bar to the other in midair. The artist must let go of the one to grab onto the other.

I let the inmates know there have been many others, in fact, the vast majority of those polled, who have sat in churches for years and never been truly touched by the truth, love, mercy, and power of God. In fact, Peter says we have all been "given everything pertaining to life and godliness" (2 Pet. 1:3). It is our choice whether or not to answer the call and engage in something more than mere words.

Judas Iscariot was chosen by God to be personally taught by Jesus, to witness Jesus' miracles for three years, and to walk with Jesus as closely as the other disciples. The tragedy of Judas' life is that he was not willing to submit his will to that of Jesus. Judas was focused on the overthrow of the Roman government. He wanted nothing to do with Jesus' talk of submission and servanthood. After Jesus was condemned to death, Judas regretted what he had done, and he hung himself. Life for him became so painful, death was the only escape he could think of. Likewise, when feeling the guilt and shame of sin in its many forms, people today often medicate with drugs, alcohol, food, or pornography. These provide brief respites only to be followed by increased guilt and shame.

The third encounter was with Peter after he denied Jesus. This one involves compassion, love, and hope for a trusted disciple—much the same as the father of the prodigal with his son when he temporarily went astray. Jesus pursued Peter to restore him to fellowship with Himself and then to send Peter out to feed His sheep. Though he had denied Christ three times, in John 21:15–25, Peter is gently led in affirming his love and devotion to Jesus. Peter faithfully served Jesus for the rest of his life. When you confess and repent of your sin, like Peter, you can be reconciled and brought back into fellowship with God!

I ask the men if they are willing to accept the Lord's love and forgiveness. Are they willing to ask the Lord for His mercy? Do they want their life to be different? Are they willing to change their attitude about themselves and see themselves as sons whom God loves? I reassure them that Jesus is reaching out His hand and wants to give them His gift of love, forgiveness, and mercy. Then I ask them if they are ready to accept new life in Christ.

What Is a Christian?

As for what it means to be a Christian, I have already discussed most of that up to this point. I let the men know that both the costs and the rewards of being a Christian are fully encompassed in one word: love. To follow Jesus, we pursue a love relationship with God and others. Doing this requires very intentional actions such as taking the risk, like Jesus did, of loving messed up people—perhaps people they do not really want to love. Love is not a feeling; it is an act of our will. The same principle is true for forgiveness and mercy.

In addition, we must see ourselves as God sees us. As for all of our past transgressions, and most prison inmates have buckets of them, once again, 2 Corinthians 5:17 tells us, "We are new creatures. Behold, the former things *have passed away* and all things have become new!" (emphasis added). Therefore, we can accept the forgiveness of God for us, and also share that forgiveness with others.

I always conclude my discussion on what is a Christian with the following invitation: "I am calling each of you, in the name of Jesus Christ, to be His follower." I want to extend my invitation to you, the readers, as well. My prayer is that you accept God's gift of salvation. I assure you that God is holding out His arms to receive you, if you ask Him to be your Lord and Savior.

Footprints in the Sand

The purpose for this talk is to help my brothers in green become more open and vulnerable to the other members of their family, and to help them realize how God is not only with them now but has been with them all their lives, even in their times of trouble. This is very difficult for some of them. Instead of making suggestions of how they can look back and see signs of God being there during those times, I wait to see if any of their other brothers in green offer their observations of how they saw God with that person during those hard times. This is what opens the door for the brothers in green to minister to one another. This creates a foundational need for Share and Prayer grouping that is highly encouraged in their walk with the Lord.

I like telling the story about a person who was walking on a sandy beach with God. At one point, the person stops and looks back at his life, represented by the footprints left in the sand. There were two sets of footprints, side by side, one was the person's and one was God's. But then, the person notices that during the times in his life when he faced great adversity, pain, and disappointment, there was only one set of footprints. Turning to God, he asks why God abandoned him when he needed Him the most. God smiled and said, "My child, I did not abandon you in your most desperate times; it was then that I picked you up and carried you."

At this point I share my storyline with my brothers in green, when my life felt much like the person in that story. I conclude by testifying how when I look back on my life, I can see where God walked with me and where He carried me, even before I knew Him as my Lord. I share how God was with me not only in those difficult times—such as the near-death experiences, the mugging that took my eyesight, and going through my divorce—but I share the positive moments also. Those events include walking away from those near-death experiences, getting my degree, finding purpose in life through prison ministry, realizing that losing my eyesight was a blessing in disguise, getting jobs with places I never wanted to work at, and meeting my wife. I tie all this together by telling my brothers that God had been molding me my whole life and keeping me alive just to serve Him by serving my brothers in green there in prison.

I instruct them to reflect on how God has touched their hearts on the retreat, how He may have cheered them on, cried over their pain, held them close, protected them, closed and opened doors, and loved them regardless of their circumstances. After they complete this exercise, I have them discuss their storyline with their fellow brothers in green at their tables and how they can now see where God was with them the whole time. If they cannot see where God was carrying them during any of those tough times, I encourage their fellow brothers to help them see where God was present. This exercise is very valuable in building a strong community of support for new believers in Christ.

Lighting the Way

The purpose of this talk is to encourage all those attending to follow up with their walk with the Lord by coming to the half-day reunions held on the second Saturday of each month. We also discuss the mountaintop-experience phenomenon and how they will soon have to go back to everyday life there in the prison. Amazing, how even in a Level IV state prison, men can actually have a mountaintop experience with Christ. But that is what happens when our God shines His light into the darkness!

I tell them their ability to experience spiritual growth is up to them, with the help of the Holy Spirit and their spiritual community there at LCF. I encourage them to lean upon the insiders at the prison, but I also caution them that no one can grow for them. One of the main differences between religion and faith in Christ is that one is a social pursuit that makes churchgoers of us, while the other is a personal relationship with Jesus.

I use the example of what I learned about the redwood forests during my bike tours in hopes it will help them understand the importance of the supporting community there at LCF. If they hope to grow in their new faith in Christ, they need to support one another. I encourage them to continue to pray and read Scripture together. This is why the Apostle Paul says we are "to be transformed by the renewing of our minds" to know and prove God's will in our lives (Rom. 12:2).

Another way I approach this talk is to first tell my brothers a short story of a few young men fishing in the evening close to the shore. When a storm started to roll in, the wind picked up, and the darkness increased along with the size and power of the waves. They became disoriented and could not figure out which way to steer their boat. Fearing for their lives, they did not know what to do until they saw the reassuring light from the lighthouse that led them back to safe harbor. Then I have a volunteer read from Romans 8:38–39, "For I am convinced that neither death nor life, neither angels nor demons, neither the present nor the future, nor any powers, neither height nor depth, nor anything else in all creation, will be able to separate us from the love of God."

The story about the young men fishing, the storm, and the lighthouse is not just a nice story, but it describes the nature of our journey. You know where you want to end up—in the safe harbor with Jesus—but the world around you is a dark and stormy place. There are so many distractions, disappointments, confusion, so much hate and anger. In the midst of all of this, how do I focus on Jesus? I remind them of the power of the Holy Spirit in them, of all the resources available to them, as well as our incredible inside team that served us and them so well and so unselfishly as living examples. They have found joy, hope, and purpose in a place no one would associate with such terms, and so can anyone who knows Jesus as Lord!

Sending Us Forth

Jesus' final words to the Twelve were "You did not choose me; no, I chose you" (John 15:16). I let my brothers know the reason they are on this three-day retreat is because Jesus invited them. God brought each of us together for a purpose. It is my prayer that they encounter Jesus in a new way at this retreat.

We demonstrate God's love to our brothers through what we do and say. The inside team waits on them hand and foot, we show love and forgiveness to one another, and we tell them God loves them and wants to forgive them of any sins they have committed. This is always a mountaintop experience for me, and my brothers in green usually feel the same way. It would be great if we could stay on this mountaintop forever, but this experience is meant to prepare us for what God is calling us to do in the valley of daily life.

Our effectiveness requires our living in union with Jesus. In John 15:5 Jesus says, "I am the vine; you are the branches. The one who remains in Me and I in him produces much fruit, because you can do nothing without Me." Only if His Spirit flows freely through us, can we bear fruit. John 14:12 states, "I tell you most solemnly, whoever believes in Me will perform the same works as I do Myself; he will perform even greater works." In Him we can do the impossible. Bearing fruit is the mark of a true follower of Jesus Christ. Jesus states, "It is to the glory of My Father that you should bear much fruit, and then you will be My disciples" (John 15:8). All we have to do is to bear witness to what we now know to be true about Jesus' victory over sin and death. We do not have to win the victory; all we have to do is to proclaim it. Jesus said, "Take courage, I have overcome the world!" (John 16:33).

Being part of the body of Christ requires ongoing surrender to the will of God, self-reflection about our relationship with the Lord, and our active participation as disciples of Christ to those we come in contact with. The call of Christ is to action. Actions do speak louder than words. The most effective way to attract people to the Lord is by our actions.

We encourage them to continue their journey by building the body of Christ and becoming part of the Prayer and Share family of Ekklesia. We stress the importance of community with our brothers in green perhaps more than anything else, because we all need the encouragement that is found in community, whether in prison or on the outside.

When the Messages Stopped

In 2020 the Covid-19 pandemic arrived, and the world, including prisons, shut down to outside programs. When you find your divine purpose, nothing compares, and having mine ripped from me was more difficult than I could have imagined. The Apostle Paul tells us in Romans 12:1 that presenting our bodies as living and holy sacrifices is our "spiritual service of worship." When we touch others in the Spirit, and not out of a sense of duty or responsibility, our physical service actually becomes as much a part of our life as anything else.

However, good news came in August of 2021 in the form of a notice from the Department of Corrections (DOC). They were going to start letting volunteers come back into the prisons if everyone had had their vaccinations and was tested the week before entering. Turned out it did not matter, because the DOC postponed entry for a couple more months. Then they took it to an entirely different level, requiring each volunteer to sign the federal government's Covid Guidelines Agreement, which had to be inspected and approved before entrance to its facilities would be granted. This made it extremely difficult to engage our volunteers as many of them objected to what they perceived to be overreaching government control and mandates to receive vaccinations they considered suspect. Overall, it was just my worst nightmare come to pass.

Nonetheless, God was in control, and when that day finally came for our return to LCF, it was one of the best ever for both us and our brothers in green because we had not been able to team up with them for almost two years. The warden and staff let us know it was a momentous day for them as well because they recognized our impact on the inmates, which helped them do their jobs. After spending nearly forty years of my life immersed in this ministry, I felt a profound loss of focus and destiny when I was not spending regular time with my brothers behind bars. Many times, you do not appreciate what you love until you lose it. Oh yes, it was good to be back!

Nevertheless, due to the continuing need for current Covid-19 tests, I was constantly concerned we would not have enough volunteers to hold a reunion. Talk about herding cats! I was constantly on the phone and emailing, reminding the guys to make sure they got out the week prior to the events so they could get their test results back in time for them to go. Sigh! There were always one or two who would get left behind because they waited too long. I found it far easier being patient with people when I considered how patient the Lord always is with me. I once heard a joke about what a sense of humor God had in letting us raise children so we could see how He felt raising a few billion of His own!

In August of 2022, we received some wonderful news, as the captain of the guard at LCF called to inform me we could do a three-day weekend retreat with our brothers in green the following October—our first in three years! They had dropped all former vaccinations and Covid-19 testing requirements, and we were good to go. We had a number of volunteers who had refused vaccination, and so I let them know the doors to LCF were open to them once more. Finally, on the last weekend in October of that year, we made up for lost time with our brothers in green who had come to mean so much to us.

As of the writing of this book, I am still, after forty-two years, deeply involved in Ekklesia Ministry. The years fly by when you find God's place for you, but the memories and the souls God has touched remain. I look forward to the day I hear God say, "Well done, good and faithful servant." In the end, it is a satisfaction you cannot possibly put a price upon.

Chapter IV:

FOUR-FOOTED GUIDANCE

No story of family or relationships would be complete without telling you about my loving, dedicated, hard-working four-footed friends I have had the honor and privilege of knowing through the years. The trust, respect, and love I have felt for my guides is hard to explain. It is intense and personal. They are not only my eyes; they are also my 24/7 companion. This intense love and respect I have for my furry partner brings an equal amount of pain when he or she passes away. I have experienced this cycle of life many times over the years, the first of which was with Gordy.

In 1981, I was without any hope of ever being able to see again; but never one to give up, I decided it was time to look into using a guide dog. I needed a pair of trained eyes guiding me and watching out for hazards. I also realized that I might be more visible to motorists if I had a dog. Perhaps, after all, there was a way to protect my face and my eyes from any more trauma. During the application process, I was asked what breed of dog I wanted, and I let it be known that I preferred a golden retriever. Even so, they informed me that the match of the dog to my needs would be the primary factor in the selection process, not the breed, but that they would try to honor my request.

Gordy

I received an announcement before the end of the year that I had been accepted into the Guide Dog program. This required me to fly out to San Rafael, California, the first week in January for the joint training of me and my dog. I spent four weeks there, graduating on January 31, 1981, with my first guide, a golden retriever named Gordy. Gordy turned out to be one of the most amazing guides that I could ever imagine having, and we became fast friends!

The following year Gordy would help me through one of the most challenging times in my life, when I found myself unemployed and very concerned about the prospects of a satisfying career. To this day I believe Gordy's presence helped me get the job at Petro Lewis in March of 1982. (Refer to Chapter VII, My Miracle Job.) In 1985 I got laid off from Petro Lewis because of the oil crash. Once again God came through, and I got another job almost immediately with the AFAFC (Air Force Accounting and Finance Center), where Gordy would have a significant impact on everyone he came in contact with.

During Gordy's career, I observed that he was not only an awesome guide, but he was a great therapy dog as well. He had a knack for sensing when anyone around me was stressed out and needed some sympathy from his big brown eyes and/or some fur to pet. With knowing compassion, he would gently lay his head in the lap of anyone having a rough day. Some people prefer no one touch their guide dogs, but it was not so with me. I loved interacting with the people Gordy led me to, and he always got a good hug out of it too.

One of his awesome traits was how intuitive he was. Without me telling him, Gordy always seemed to know where I was going, whether it was to work, church, or to Wendy's restaurant. He loved going to church to hang out with all the people who doted over him; and, amazingly, he always seemed to sense the day and the hour it was time to go. We also attended my Men's Full-Gospel prayer breakfast regularly on Wednesday morning before going to work. It was obvious he looked forward to this, because instead of going to the bus stop on those mornings; he sat outside of our gate, where Pastor Jack picked us up.

In 1989 Gordy developed hip dysplasia and was having trouble going up and down the stairs at work, which led me to face the end of our very special relationship. Retiring him as a guide dog also had a significant impact around work at the AFAFC (Air Force Accounting and Finance Center). The management team decided to throw an elaborate retirement ceremony for Gordy in December, featuring guest speakers, the Director of the AFAFC, and several commanding officers. Gordy was center stage on a new bed, which was only one of the gifts he received. His many friends packed the auditorium to say farewell to their favorite mascot.

Early in 1990, I decided it was time to find a new home for Gordy. Much as it saddened me, the old boy could not do his job anymore. Besides all that, my work and my activities kept me from the house around fourteen hours a day. Gordy still wanted to work for me and did not understand why he was being left behind. It broke my heart to leave home every day and hear his whimpers coming from behind the door. He needed a new home where people would give him the time and attention I used to.

Mickey's sister had a special relationship with Gordy and took care of him often whenever we were gone, so I offered him to her. She initially took him but then turned around and gave him to one of her daughters. This was fine with me because she assured me Gordy was in a good home.

Lassen

In March of that year, I went to San Rafael to get my second guide dog, Lassen—again a golden retriever that turned out to be another amazing partner. When I returned from San Rafael with Lassen, I repacked my bags and immediately went to Snowmass with a friend named Julie, who played the violin. With me playing guitar, we made quite the bluegrass duo as we played for nursing home residents around the Denver area. Julie also doubled as my cross-country ski guide while we were in Snowmass.

Just like Gordy, his predecessor, Lassen had no problem warming up to the folks at work and the staff at the hotels we stayed at. We never had any problem finding people to watch him while we were out carving up the snow. Life was good, and I was starting to heal from the loss of Gordy and Mickey, the two friends who had been closest to me up to that point. There was nothing that helped me get over the passing of one of my trusted four-footed friends more than getting to know and love a new one.

When we went back to Topeka the first week in June of 1992 for our Regional NBBA Tournament (National Beep Baseball Association), I borrowed a friend's van so Lassen and six of us could travel together. It was great to have Yvonne along as our new designated driver. For one of us to be "driving blind" or under the influence was not wise. I knew, for I had tried both.

On our way back from Topeka, we stopped in Burlington to fuel up the van. We had the doors open because everyone went in and out for restroom breaks and food. This incident reminded me of the story in the Bible where Jesus' parents were on their way home from Jerusalem when someone asked, "Where is Jesus?" What prompted this was someone in the back of the van asking me, "Where is Lassen?" just as we were leaving the station! Apparently, he got out of the van without anyone noticing. Well, a dog's gotta take a potty break too. When Yvonne looked in the rearview mirror, she saw Lassen, my trusted guide dog, wandering around the gas pumps. We turned around and went back to the gas station. Lassen was casually sniffing his way around, seemingly without a care in the world! We all got a good laugh out of that one.

Moments like this constantly reminded me of God's faithfulness in watching over His children. Considering the only sighted person in the van was Yvonne, and with her being concerned with driving and possibly not noticing Lassen's absence for many miles, God chose one of the sightless among us to "see" Lassen was missing. When you consider the many places I have gone during my life with my dogs, I am happy to say none have been hurt or lost. The big takeaway of this trip was not what Lassen was up to but that Yvonne was a big hit with everyone, fitting right into her first-ever Beep Baseball Tournament.

My life with Lassen went on, mostly consisting of baseball, skiing, bike riding, and the prison ministry until, in the spring of 1998, I found out my trusted four-legged friend had cancer and was refusing to eat his food. I knew it was time to put him down, but I just could not bring myself to do it, so I asked Yvonne to take him to the vet. Afterward, I realized that it was a very selfish act on my part because Yvonne loved Lassen just as much as I did. Nonetheless, the sadness of this moment was one mountain, blind or otherwise, I just could not summit. Still, life goes on and I needed a new guide dog, so I applied for another four-footed guide, and in August of that year, I went back to California to meet my new friend Dixon.

Dixon

Dixon was another great guide dog who, along with Gordy, were the two most dedicated guide dogs I have owned over my life. They both seemed to be able to read my mind and know what my next command would be before I even spoke it. People used to say Dixon worshipped me because he would never leave my side, even when I took his harness and leash off. That had its disadvantages because he could never relax and just play with other dogs. I felt like he truly had no interests other than serving me.

Yet there was one other role he filled, and that was cleaning the floors at the Prodigal Coffee House, where I was ministering to troubled youth from the streets of Denver (more on this in chapter VII). It was a safe place where they could hang out and hear the gospel. Dixon was very well known for ensuring the floors were cleaned up from all the popcorn we served to the kids. There was a standing joke that it took a lot longer to clean up the floors when Dixon was not there!

As was inevitable though, while on a bike tour event in 2007, I received a call from Yvonne to let me know that another one of my beloved dogs had cancer. She asked me what I wanted to do, and I said to wait until I got home, and we would take him to an animal hospital for a second opinion. When we took him in for further diagnostics, they were able to clearly see a tumor in his abdomen. Even though he had cancer, Dixon still wanted to do his job every day, so I continued to take him with me to work. He persevered for another year.

My last hurrah with him was taking him to a barbeque where many of the HeartCycle riders who had finished the first leg of the Ride Across America Tour would be. Dixon had become good friends with many of them over the years, and I thought it would be a good opportunity for all of them to say goodbye and to let him know how much he was loved. When we arrived home that evening, he got out of the car and wanted to go to the backyard. He lay down in the grass, and I could not get him to come into the house. I went out and sat with him for a couple of hours before I went to bed. When I awoke the next day, he had not moved, which confirmed that the sun was setting for him. It was off to the vet again for that appointment I hated so much.

Anyone who has had to put down a faithful four-legged friend knows the emotions that tear at you. On the one hand, you do not want to see them suffer and know it is best to end it, but then there is the voice crying inside you, "No, give me just a bit more time with him!" In my case—which is especially true because of the special bond between me and my trusted, furry partners—I found myself sitting on the floor at the vet's office with Dixon's head in my lap. Something in our special communication told me he knew what was coming, and it was okay. Ah, Dixon, guiding me to the very end. This was the third time I had to say goodbye to one of my dogs.

This makes me think about another "goodbye." I imagine God grieves too when one of His children buys into worldliness and pride, and He has to say to them, "Goodbye, I wish you had loved Me as I loved you, because then we could have been together forever." I know it breaks His heart.

With Dixon being gone, I needed to call Guide Dogs in California to let them know about Dixon's passing and to request they put me on the waiting list for another golden retriever. I thought it would be a long time before one would become available, but then I serve a miraculous Provider. In just two weeks, Guide Dogs called and said they had a guide for me, a female named Lizzie. Since my previous guides were all males, they were concerned whether I was okay with having a female guide. When I hung up the telephone and told Yvonne I wanted to think about it, I did not even need to hear her objections or see the look on her face. I could feel the heat! So, I called Guide Dogs back to give them my approval. They told me they would make the arrangements for me to fly to Oregon for two weeks of training with my new guide.

Lizzie

I like to think of the call from Guide Dogs as another one of those divine appointments. Lizzie was fully trained, yet the director made the decision to hold her for "someone" who wanted a dog with a faster pace. That would be me. When I arrived at the school, I learned Lizzie was special in another way. She had been rescued as a pup from a home where the owners were meth dealers. One evening during a police raid, there was a fire and Lizzie suffered severe burns. One of the officers called one of their own, Lori, who was known for rescuing dogs. It was initially not known whether Lizzie would survive or not; but after the veterinarian released her, Lori took Lizzie home and loved her back to health. Lori gave this abused little pup a second chance in life!

Moreover, we serve a God of second chances. He takes those who have been badly burned by the world and sin, gathers them up into His arms, heals them, and gives them a reason to hope again. I say, "AMEN!" If you are looking, you will see God's hand in so many of life's circumstances.

After a few months, Lori donated Lizzie to the guide dog program. Lizzie was a high-energy natural leader, with a faster-than-normal pace. She quickly earned the nickname "Road Runner" because she always passed up any other guide team that was ahead of her. "Hmm," Yvonne would say, "Does that sound like anyone we know?" After returning to Colorado with Lizzie, I learned to keep a firm grip on her harness because for her to be in motion meant full speed ahead. In stepping off a bus, the moment her paws hit the sidewalk, she was off to the races. Even in play, Lizzie took pleasure in running at top speed, and after a good run came back to us with a huge smile on her face.

Lizzie became a powerful testimony to my brothers in green when we went to the prison, because all those guys needed a second chance, just like she had experienced.

Maureen, the lady Lizzie was assigned to in the guide dog program, and her husband, Dave, lived near the coast in Oregon and loved to fish for salmon and tuna. Shortly after I took Lizzie home to Colorado, they came out to visit family and contacted us. After enticing them with some of my famous homemade ice cream (if the blind guy with the guide dog does not win them over, the blind guy with the ice cream usually does), they asked me to join them in fishing for tuna.

While recovering from rotator cuff surgery in 2010, I got a call from Maureen to invite me to come back to Oregon City for some tuna fishing in July. I thought this would be good therapy for my shoulder, so I agreed. Lizzie and I flew to Portland, where Maureen picked us up from the airport. Our first stop was Parkin's Electric, where Maureen worked and Lizzie received much of her social training. Maureen's coworkers were looking forward to seeing Lizzie again, and Lizzie was excited to see them as well. As I addressed questions about how I lost my sight, I was able to share my testimony with some of them.

From there, we went to our hosts' home, where Lizzie got reacquainted with her favorite aforementioned donkey. Early the next morning we headed out to Lincoln near Depo Bay, where Dave's mother lived right on the ocean shoreline. From there, we went out in their beautiful cabin cruiser over fifty miles from their dock to get to the cold, deep water where tuna hang out. Despite my excitement at the prospect of catching true fighting fish that weigh around thirty pounds, it was just not our day. Nevertheless, I did have an opportunity to do fishing of another sort, for Dave had some clients with us in the boat, and I got to cast a different sort of net in Jesus' name. I have always shared my testimony anywhere and everywhere I can. All in all, it was a great experience, and one more check off my bucket list.

As 2017 unfolded, I realized in early spring that Lizzie was slowing down to the point that I felt she wanted to retire. So, I went back to the good folks who had supplied my former guides to let them know I wanted to be put on the list for another golden retriever. A few weeks later, they called me back and asked if I would be willing to accept a mixed-breed golden. I was hopeful my new guide would have better health than a purebred. So, in May, it was back to San Rafael, California, to get my fifth guide dog: a cross between a golden and a yellow Lab. Her name is Nicolina, and I soon found out she is easily distracted by other dogs and food.

Nicolina

Everybody told me she was cute as a button. Each of my guides has been unique and special. It is hard not to love a dog you count on and are with 24/7. For the first time, we had two guide dogs in our home, plus Yvonne's pet golden, Pearl. Fortunately, a couple of our friends had grown quite fond of Lizzie, and she them; so, when we had to leave town with Nicolina, we knew retired Lizzie would be in good hands with our friends. Then it occurred to me, why not ask our friends if they would consider adopting Lizzie full-time? That way, there would be no competition between the two dogs, and we could visit her any time we wanted. When I suggested this arrangement, our friends readily agreed, and so, in July of 2017, Lizzie went off to her new home.

Unfortunately, a mere two months later, Lizzie's health quickly failed, to the point that she could hardly walk. We took her to the animal hospital, where they discovered cancer throughout her body with a tumor the size of a softball in her abdomen. Once again, it was time to put down a faithful friend.

As of the printing of this book, Nicolina is my eyes. I look forward to many good times with her in the years to come, and I treasure the many memories of my earlier guides.

Chapter V:

BACKSEAT DRIVER

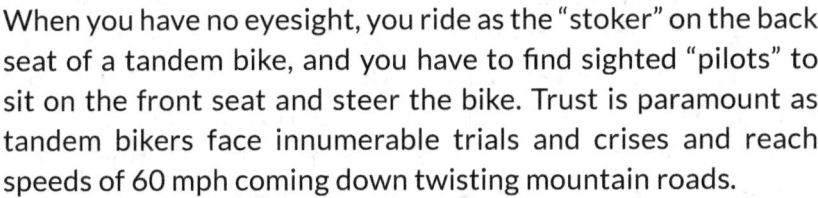

When you have no eyesight, you ride as the "stoker" on the back seat of a tandem bike, and you have to find sighted "pilots" to sit on the front seat and steer the bike. Trust is paramount as tandem bikers face innumerable trials and crises and reach speeds of 60 mph coming down twisting mountain roads.

My first cycling tour began in the summer of 1989 when I signed up to ride the first Pedal the Peaks Tour held in Colorado. Cycling became one of the most fertile fields, along with the prisons, for sharing my testimony. Over the next thirty-five years, I toured with Bicycle Tours of Colorado, HeartCycle, Ride Across Wyoming (RAW), and Register's Annual Great Bicycle Ride Across Iowa (RAGBRAI)—crossing over sixty major mountain passes across the United States.

Referring to the Pedal the Peaks Tour, I could not get anyone to take the whole week to pilot my tandem bike, so we had to start halfway through the tour in Gunnison. That first tour was a disaster, since I was clueless as to what would be demanded of us. My pilot, James, was Pastor Jack's grandson. He was just fourteen years old and more clueless than I was. We trained for all of one day, riding for forty miles on flat streets; but being me, I figured that would do. Were we in for a big surprise! On the first day out from Gunnison to Buena Vista, we headed up Monarch

Pass, where we faced a twenty-four-mile climb. James was not familiar with the derailleur on my bike, which caused us no end of grief trying to make it to the summit. I imagined the other cyclists mumbling "rookies" under their breath as they passed by.

The next day, as we rode from Buena Vista to Frisco, James proved to me just how capable he was. When we reached the summit of Fremont Pass it started raining, and it continued to rain most of the way into Frisco. That evening, when we were sitting in a hot tub at the hotel, James explained how the wet rims of the wheels made the caliper brakes virtually useless most of the way down the mountain. Another challenge was avoiding cars coming up the mountain in our bike lane, forcing him to ride the white line next to the road's edge most of the way down the pass. I surmised that the only thing that saved us, besides God Himself, was the disc brakes. (God can use anything, even disc brakes, to accomplish His purposes.) The valuable lessons aided me in purchasing my future tandems. He told me he did not say anything during the ride because he did not want me to be afraid of what was going on. He evidently was not aware of my history with bikes, cars, and on roads, or he would have been the one freaking out!

Through all our trials—which included misaligned and blown tires, brakes malfunctioning, flooded streets that threatened to sweep us away, and assorted self-inflicted wounds—we did not exactly compete. However, I know neither of us would trade that experience for anything, and we can look back on it now and have a good laugh.

You often straddle a fine line between enduring and collapsing; the weather does not cooperate, you experience both good and bad organizers that can seriously affect the trip, and there are days when you just want to give up and go back home. In those times, I remember the God who has given me such a wonderful life and His exhortations to do all I do with excellence for His sake (Col. 3:23). I also remember the trials Jesus endured for my sake that make mine look trivial and, as the Apostle Paul says, "I press on" (Philippians 3:12) for His glory!

Riding is not only a love of my life, but it is good for me physically. Seeing this would be a lifelong passion of mine, Yvonne signed up to be a volunteer for many of my tours. A perk that resulted was while the riders did not enjoy overnight hotel rooms, the volunteers did, so I did not have to camp out—enjoying God's creation all day while riding was enough nature appreciation for this old farmhand. At night, I was ready for those creature comforts man has developed and time with the companion God has given me.

RB and his longtime pilot: Nate

My blindness has served as a platform to tell people what God has done in my life— not only in the prisons but also during my cycling tours, when I travel through airports, sit in hotel lobbies, on buses, or in taxis. People will always inquire about my blindness, typically asking me when and how it happened or if I have been blind since birth. When I tell them my story of the mugging that took what little sight I had, they always respond with, "Oh, that is terrible!" Then I tell them I thought so too at first, but I came to realize it was a blessing in disguise. Of course, they are quite confused, which opens the door for me to give them my testimony. I tell them what God has done in my life, how He totally turned my life around to "walk by faith, not by sight," and how that radically altered the way I have lived and the incredible opportunities I have experienced. I could never have known any of it without "that tragic night."

Riding in the RAW

When June of 2000 rolled around, a friend and one of my part-time bike pilots, whom I worked with, talked me into going on a tour called Ride Across Wyoming (their slogan is "Ride in the RAW"), which was sponsored by a church in Sheridan and kicked off in Jackson Hole. You would think the arduous miles put in under my feet would be the biggest challenge on these tours; but the truth is finding and keeping good pilots, who were willing to leave families and work for weeks at a time, was a bigger challenge. My friend let me know up front that he did not want to pilot my tandem through the entire tour, so on the first day we arrived there, we put a note up on the bulletin board asking if anybody would be interested in the position. If someone was interested but had not piloted a tandem before, we even offered to train them.

The next day a guy named Nate Dick, a man who would end up being my friend and pilot for years to come, responded to the note. Nate's talent was immediately recognizable, and even my friend from work realized my experience was going to be much better with Nate at the helm. In fact, on the downhill side of the Grand Tetons Pass, I was hoping to break my speed record of 70 mph with my new and immensely talented pilot; but unfortunately, the local police had other ideas and held us under 40 mph.

One night on this ride, when we were at a bar and I was sitting at a table talking to some of the other cyclists, the barmaid came up to me and asked me if I was coming back later that night. Being confused by the question, I asked if there was some reason that she would ask that. She replied, "Because I am gonna kick your butt!" Now I was really confused and asked what I had done to merit a butt-kicking, thinking I had put those years behind me. Apparently, my friend from work had told her that I was something akin to Minnesota Fats (for you young people out there, he was a famous hustler and pool shark). Turns out she was the town pool shark, and we all laughed when she explained that my friend had told her my cane was actually a pool cue that I took everywhere with me. Beep Pool? I don't think so.

The smashing point of the RAW story was, once again, God coming through in a way I could never have hoped or imagined. Here I was on a tour I had never been on before and had to be talked into, with a pilot who was really ready to call it quits, and God brought a man to me who knew nothing of piloting, needed training, and lived up in the mountains of Colorado where I would never have just run into him. And yet, this man ended up being a great friend and the best, most enduring pilot I ever had.

Nate later asked me to go back to Wyoming and ride over what they call The Big Horn, a sister mountain range to the Rockies. The Big Horn was a tough ride with a long uphill eastern climb and a fast descent down the western slope. Thinking I would tempt fate one more time just for kicks, we found ourselves cruising the downward slope at around 55 mph when we started drifting into the oncoming traffic lanes. Suddenly, Nate started yelling, "Lean harder, Ron! Lean harder!" As we both did, Nate barely brought the bike back into our lane before I heard a car pass us going the other way! The Lord was certainly watching over us that day.

One of the funny things that occurred during the Big Horn Tour was one of the volunteers who offered to help pilot me for a leg of it was a motorcyclist, and he dressed more for that occasion than as a bicyclist. We looked pretty silly: me on the back seat with my spandex and all, and him on the front seat with a motorcycle helmet, jean shorts, and cowboy boots! Despite the apparel that drew laughs from riders and spectators alike, he actually did quite a good job.

Doing My Own Thing

2003 was a slow year for bicycle tours, and being the primary fundraiser for our beep baseball team, I needed to come up with something new to replace the donation pledges for the number of miles I would ride. I came up with my own tour of a different sort around Colorado. I wanted it to extend 500 miles over several days, with several new people piloting my bike to expose them to the sport. The route included the Denver metro area and several surrounding cities, like Aurora and Westminster, and of course my old haunt: Limon.

The day that reminded me most of the mountain tours wound its way through the foothills (a route they call "the Lariat" because, from a satellite view it resembles a cowboy's lariat laying on the ground) to Evergreen, down past the world-renowned Red Rocks Amphitheater, through Morrison, and then along C-470 back to my house. This was no big deal for me, whom some of my friends had started to call "the indomitable one." It would be hard to think of a greater compliment people could give me. I was able, through this effort, to keep the funds coming in for my beep baseball team.

RAGBRAI

In 2005 one of my other veteran pilots, Chris, told me my twenty-year-old bike was showing its age and, worse, was becoming increasingly difficult to find parts for. He was afraid that if it broke down at some critical point in the season, we might miss events because of a lack of parts to fix it. So, I began my search for a new steed in my hometown of Littleton. It just so happened the national sales rep from the Trek corporation was visiting a store at the same time Yvonne and I came in. Given the miles I rode and the terrain I encountered, he convinced us we needed a top-of-the-line, special-order bike. At first I hesitated, but Yvonne argued that this would be the last tandem I would ever buy, so why not get the best? We splurged, and I have never regretted it. The new Trek made my old bike feel like a refugee from a junkyard and made all those mountain passes somehow a little less bumpy.

With my sweet new Trek Tandem under us, Chris suggested we take on the Register's Annual Great Bicycle Ride Across Iowa (RAGBRAI). It just so happened that this ride would be going close to the home of my son-in-law's parents in Algona, which would provide a perfect mix of sport and family time. There were many cool traditions that went along with the tour, among them the custom of putting our rear wheels in the Missouri River on the west side of Iowa, where the tour began, and then putting our front wheels in the Mississippi River when we got to the east side of Iowa at the finish line.

The RAGBRAI provides a significant economic boost for the state of Iowa. You could not go more than a few miles without running into vendors like Mr. Pork Chop, selling whatever food or other supplies they specialized for cyclists and spectators.

It was God's protection that we were sleeping in homes of host families on the Iowa tour because of the regular severe storms that rolled through the Midwest. It seemed that every year, there was at least one night of meteorological mayhem. Sadly, one year a participant was killed when a large tree branch came down on his tent. Even me, the guy who survived being hit by a 26,000-pound RTD bus, could not have survived that one.

The next year I did the RAGBRAI for the second time, except this time around Nate piloted my tandem. On this tour we rode across the southern part of Iowa, which involved a lot more climbing. On the last day of the tour, and after we dipped the front tire in the Mississippi River, Nate unclipped his feet from the pedals and stuck them up in the air for a funny photo, while I took charge of pedaling up the ramp on the waterfront. After the picture was taken, I said to Nate, "Wow, that did not feel any different than the rest of the rides we have done together! Is there something you are not telling me?" We both had a good laugh at that one.

Speaking of humor, a tradition that began on the Iowa tours occurred when a couple of women who were regulars at the event passed us one day while we were taking it easy, and one exclaimed, "You have just been chicked!" From then on, it became a goal for the women to pass the men and proclaim those famous words loudly and proudly.

During that ride, Nate introduced me to several of his friends who were members of a group of 55-and-older skiers called The Ski Meisters out of Winter Park, Colorado. Nate encouraged me to join the Ski Meisters as well as the HeartCycle Bicycle Club. "Mr. never say no" rides again! With these new affiliations in hand, I had new opportunities for exciting fellowship or evangelical and recreational opportunities.

In July of 2019, I headed for Iowa to do the RAGBRAI Tour once more and to meet Jesse, my new pilot. This became an interesting situation because I could not see that the person who was in front of me was wearing a dress! It turns out he was in the process of transitioning from male to female, and I did not know it until other riders pointed out his attire to me. When they brought this up, I just commented that this was the strongest lady who had ever piloted my tandem!

Now, there might be a number of Christians out there who would be offended by being paired up with a transgender person, but knowing what my life was like before I met Christ, could I really criticize anyone for who they are apart from Him? Did not Jesus come to the confused, the outcasts, and the nobodies? Did He not look down on those shouting, "Crucify Him!" and say, "Father forgive them, they know not what they do"? (Luke 23:34). Apart from Jesus Christ, people live in a world ruled by sin, the lies of the devil, chaos, fear, and death. It is not our job to judge or criticize them. It is our job to love them and let the Holy Spirit gently show them the error of their ways, as He does with all of His children.

Once again, the Lord's protection made itself known as, on the last day of our tour, we were heading full speed toward an intersection that was supposed to be blocked but was not. Just as Jesse and I were entering the intersection, a car came through, and Jesse swerved just in time to avoid being hit! Hmm, how many lives have I used up? I lost count somewhere along the way because I know my Savior is always with me, so it did not really matter.

Moab

As 2007 began to unfold, Nate and a group from Estes Park invited me to go with them in June to Moab, Utah, for a shorter bike tour. They had rented a condo there, and each day we departed to ride a different route. One of those days, we rode out to The Arches National Park, where we hiked through a rock formation they called The Fiery Furnace next to Dead Horse Point. As far as I know, I was the first blind person ever to hike through there.

The most memorable part about that Moab trip did not occur in Moab at all. It happened on the way home when we stopped at the Colorado Monument and decided to ride that. We rode up the west side, stopped at the visitor's center, then came down on the eastern side. There were some dangerous curves there without railings that would prove fatal if missed. Sometimes, it is a blessing to be blind! Some of those curves were restricted to 25 or 30 mph for cars, but we attacked them at 45 mph all the way down. Total trust in your pilot is a necessity when doing this sort of thing, and I trusted Nate implicitly. We were both die-hard adventure junkies!

When we got back to the van after riding that pass, some people we were riding with noticed my rear tire was flat. Upon further examination, we found it was worn clear through the rubber, had destroyed the threads, and was into the tube itself. Want to believe in God's protection? Try riding down a mountain pass with steep, unprotected curves at 15–20 mph over the posted speed limit, only to find your rear tire could have blown out at any moment! Nate's memorable quote to me as we stood there looking at what probably should have killed us both was, "Ron, this is why I love riding with you. I know God is watching over you."

Crisscrossing America I: The Ride Across America!

In 2007, I heard from a friend named Jerry that a plan to ride across the southern United States with HeartCycle was in the works. As many places as I had been on my tandem, this was one trip that was still on my bucket list, so I responded to the invitation to participate with an emphatic "Yes!" Unfortunately, the board of the club did not have the same enthusiasm Jerry and I shared. However, Jerry kept pursuing it by asking every member of the organization he knew to petition the board to change their minds. His persistence paid off, and the board finally agreed to add the tour to the 2008 list. We called it the RAAT (Ride Across America Tour). When we arrived in San Diego, our SAG (support and gear) van drivers were there and raring to go! The vans were used to carry parts, food, water, and also to transport stranded cyclists. These two female drivers, who took care of my every need, were lovingly nicknamed the Texas Tornadoes. Our tour would be a mix of riding and rest days for two weeks each year, for a period of three years, and end up on the beach in St. Augustine, Florida.

When I was having trouble securing a pilot for the first leg of the journey, Jerry volunteered for the job. We had put too much into making this happen for him to leave me behind. Talk about commitment! Thirty-six of us met for what began as a three-year commitment yet actually ended up being considerably longer for me, if you included all the time I spent working as a volunteer registrar for the organization. The head registrar resigned a couple of years later and I took his spot; a position I held for approximately fifteen years.

Over the first five days, we put in about 450 miles, with a mixture of steep inclines with snow on them, bumps that made things interesting, long flat expanses, and some twisty downhills. There were even times we had to hitchhike because it had gotten too dark to ride safely. When we did get a lift, we had to go back the next morning to where we were picked up and restart there. El Paso marked the end of the first year of the ride, and it was where we resumed the journey in 2009.

After 121 miles on the first day of the second leg, the second day took us up 4,900 feet in elevation. Another day on that tour put us on an intercept course with a motorcycle rally in a small Texas town. As we arrived, the bikers had a huge tent set up with lots of coolers full of beer. They invited us to join them and offered us a "few cold ones," noting how impressed they were that we could do what they were doing but without engines under our butts.

Bike riding gave me a constant and considerable appetite, and I became famous on the tour for being the tall, skinny guy who could outeat everyone and never gain any weight. I ate every meal down to the plate, along with all the snacks our Texas Tornadoes offered me. Our next stop of note was in Luckenbach— you know, the one featured in the song made famous by Waylen Jennings and Willie Nelson. Because of the song, I figured we were headed to a city like Nashville and other places that were famous for music. However, Luckenbach is little more than a small amusement park with a century-old bar, an operating post office, and a small outdoor stage/amphitheater, all made out of really old wood. It was very rustic and not at all what I expected.

The rest of the trip featured climbing 20 percent grades in the rain, where our tires spun out because we were literally standing on our pedals; interfering with a local craft show, which did not sit well with the merchants; listening to frogs croak as we road through marshlands; and being treated to our first Cajun meal of the tour, featuring jambalaya, catfish, and many other tasty Cajun goodies.

To kick off 2010, I flew to Houston to start the last leg of the tour. Other riders continuously asked me why I did this. My answer was that I wanted to see the country, and I could not think of a better way to do that than by sitting on my tandem. Their response was typically what I am sure yours is now, "*See* the country?" It is hard to explain, but believe me, there are more ways to see things than with eyesight. Imagine that. And the food. Did I mention the food?

As we pedaled this last leg, the ever-present Patty was trying to "chick" us on her bike. Nate decided to play a game of possum with her, which really annoyed her. We waited until she was right up on our rear wheel, then Nate yelled back to me, "Here comes Patty!" and we took off, leaving her in the dust. This game went on from Texas to the Florida coast, and even Patty had a great time with it. Truth be told, we played possum with a lot of the riders.

We were always the last to sign out for the start every morning, but we passed up at least 50 percent of the other cyclists by the end of the day. At the end of one day of the tour, Nate overheard some other cyclists comment about how slow we were, never finishing any higher than mid-pack. We decided to show them our true colors, riding hard all the way, only spending five minutes at each of the SAG stops, and taking just twenty minutes for lunch. We smoked 'em all and never heard any comments from that group again!

Overall, the other riders were very supportive, and as we got close to our hotel in St. Augustine, people were yelling, "Go, go, go!" Some even blocked traffic because we had finished so late due to tire and wheel issues we had encountered on that last day. They were all cheering us on as if we had just won the Tour de France! When we arrived, we hurried straight for the beach to get our front tire dipped in the Atlantic Ocean because we thought everybody else had already done so. To our surprise, we found out everyone had waited for us, and no one had dipped their tires before we got there. It was champagne all around, and then everyone celebrated the finish together, knowing we had checked off one more to-do on our bucket list. At the awards dinner, the nine riders who completed every leg got a hearty standing ovation from their peers.

Once again, my Great Provider had turned lemons into lemonade and introduced me to some amazing people as well! When you are in God's will because you have made a practice of seeking it and walking in it, you are blessed by such a variety of relationships in an equally vast variety of ways. You end up just sitting back and watching Him work, knowing His plan is far better than yours, and you are in the best of hands.

Crisscrossing America II: Border-to-Border

At the annual HeartCycle board meeting and luncheon on the last Saturday in October 2010, it was announced that the next portion of the Great Adventure Tour, the Border-to-Border Tour, would start in Vancouver, Canada, and then proceed down the Pacific coast to Mexico. This new proposal was due to the success of the Ride Across America Tour. So, the following spring, I started my proverbial pilot search for it and other tours I desired to ride. While Nate was always my faithful standby, I hated to rely upon him too much, especially for the long tours like the border-to-border one coming up. We agreed Nate would pilot the longer tours for one week, but I would have to find someone for any time over that.

As always, I prayed and God provided. I met a man named Neil through a national organization I was a part of, and when he found out about the tour, he said he would gladly pilot for me. How many people do you think you would just "encounter" who would want to leave their families, fly halfway across the country, and give up riding their own bike for a two-week test of endurance and strength? However, when you walk with God, things like this happen all the time.

Thankful for the new help, there was still serious practice that needed to be completed. We found a local tour called the Tony's-to-Tony's ride, starting at Tony's Meat Market in downtown Denver, and from there we visited three of the other franchises in and around the Denver area. It was under 100 miles in length, but it would give my prospective new pilot and me a good indication of how we would sync up. Overall, it went well, and we looked forward to a great adventure together.

A few days before we would catch the flight to Vancouver, I had to take my tandem over to load it up on the SAG truck. One of the deciding factors in me entering a tour where my bike had to be transported a long distance was the availability of the SAG vehicle, due to the immense costs involved in shipping a large tandem bike. On the SAG, it would only cost me $75 instead of $500 or more on a plane; and I actually felt better about the bike's safety when the ones in charge knew me.

In addition to saving me the transport money on the bike, God bailed me out a second time on this journey because I had mistakenly bought the wrong visa. When Neil and I arrived at the gate to catch our flight, I was informed that the one I had obtained did not cover flying over the border into Canada. Fortunately, the agent at the gate was very helpful, explaining that we could get another flight into Seattle and drive the rest of the way. We took her advice and made the rider's instructional meeting in the nick of time! Everyone who had heard of our trials was shocked when we walked into that room, but I was not surprised at all. I just smiled, knowing that somehow God would work things out because He had pulled me through worse situations in my life.

On the first day, we would start our long journey south across the Canadian border into Washington State. I ascertained from a cousin there that we would be unusually blessed with fine weather. No chilly days or rain as were the norm that time of year, rather temperatures in the low 70s and dry. This ride would be a lot shorter than the one from coast to coast we had completed the previous year. After three days, we ended up in Oak Harbor, where we got a day off and enjoyed a ferry ride out to one of the San Juan Islands.

The next segment of the ride was the longest on this first two-week leg of the tour. It was a real blessing having Neil as my pilot because he took good care of me and excellent care of the bike! He spent hours every night inspecting, cleaning, waxing, and oiling it to make sure it was ready for the next day. However, as we were riding along, one of the riders following us noticed I had a broken spoke on my rear wheel. As He had done so often during my journeys, God came through with a new spoke another rider "just happened to have with him." His bike and mine were not the same manufacturer, but the spoke fit. It seemed the maintenance gremlins were never done with us.

While we were changing out the spoke, Neil noticed that I was using a heavy thorn-resistant tube and decided to change out that tube for a lightweight tube. Neil was always calculating how we could make the bike lighter. He concluded that by using the lighter-weight tire tubes instead of the heavier ones we could make the tandem a couple of pounds lighter. Unfortunately, after replacing the thorn-resistant tube with the lighter tubes, we ended up suffering five flats.

When Nate rejoined me, we decided it was time to get rid of the lighter tubes and put the heavier, thorn-resistant ones back on. We then rode into Oregon where we had a day off. We spent that day at Cannon Beach. As we were out walking through the sand, we were approached by a young lady who lived nearby and was interested in HeartCycle and what we were doing. When she learned we were from Colorado, she informed us she had gone on a ski scholarship to Western State in Gunnison, Colorado. I told her my cousin had done the very same thing, and her eyes got wide as saucers! She not only knew my cousin, but they had also been great friends, roommates, and on the same ski team together! I chalked it up to one more divine appointment, which I had come to expect on my great adventure with Jesus.

And did I mention the food? If you want to enjoy some of the world's best seafood restaurants— day after day—just travel down the northwest coast of America. For a food junkie like me, this was seafood heaven! And along with the restaurants, we visited several old lighthouses, where God always reminded me that He was my lighthouse. He would keep me off the rocky shoals and safe from any storm, as long as I kept my eyes on Him. From there it was one more day into Bandon, Oregon, where we caught a ride to the airport for the trip home.

On the second leg of the tour in 2012, I would have to find someone to pilot my tandem the week Nate could not. God came through once more as, at the Regional Ski for Light event that year, I raised concern over my lack of a pilot to the gathered regional participants and volunteers. And voila! A fellow board member and ski guide accepted the challenge!

After gathering in Eugene, Nate and I took a bus down to Bandon, where we had finished the first leg of the tour the prior year. This leg would take us through the famed redwood forests of northern California, where I learned a great deal about these massive trees, which were not only the largest in diameter but also the tallest in the world. Another incredible fact I would use in my prison talks was that the redwoods have amazingly small and shallow root systems. You would think the slightest breeze would topple such tall wonders of nature. However, they have a secret strength that keeps them upright and growing: a community root system that intertwines with all the other trees around them to make one massive, stabilizing, impenetrable mat of roots!

This community analogy is especially apropos to believers in prison, where it is critical to build a cohesive community of fellow believers to keep them upright and strong while the winds of depression, hopelessness, chaos, and fear constantly blow to try to topple them from their relationship with God. The Bible is full of references to the fact that we were created for community. We were created to love and be loved, and that simply cannot happen when your goal is to be self-sufficient. As we disciple the inmates, we always encourage them to have their brothers' backs and gather around anyone they observe giving in to temptation or falling away from the community.

The tour then took us to Fort Bragg and across the famous Golden Gate Bridge on our way to Half Moon Bay, where we finished this second leg of the tour. I arranged to have dinner with one of my favorite nieces, Brenda, who met me there. She had always wanted to train and raise guide dogs, but then life came along, and as a nurse and a mother, the time for anything more was just not there.

In late October, at the Annual HeartCycle board meeting, it was pilot hunting time once more. After the first of the following year, I got a lead for a guy from Seattle. He had led many tours up in the Cascades and often rode with his wife on their tandem, so the experience was certainly there. I called him, and, you guessed it, he agreed to pilot my tandem for the week Nate could not. I learned that we would be riding past the Hearst Castle, and we all planned a half-day break to take the tour.

On the first day of the final leg of the tour in May, we seemed to hit all four seasons of weather in under an hour. The day began under warm, sunny skies that soon turned cloudy. Then the wind started to blow. Shortly after that it started raining, which turned into snow. Then the sun came back out, and it became more spring-like. After arriving in Santa Cruz, I called my niece Brenda, who lived there, and we had dinner with some family and friends at a Mexican restaurant.

A couple of days later, the ride down to Cambria took us to the entrance to Hearst Castle, where our SAG drivers set up our lunch stop while those who had purchased tickets took the tour. We then headed to Pismo Beach, where I met up with Nate for the remainder of the ride. Our next day off was in Santa Barbara, where Nate and I went down to the waterfront and walked down the pier.

All this time, we were riding down the famous Coastal Highway 1. It took us all the way to the Mexican border and then back to San Diego on May 18, where our tour ended. Knowing I had now ridden the entire country, west to east and north to south, was rewarding. Who would think that a crazy blind kid from Colville could accomplish this much? However, I know if I had kept my sight, the chances of any of it happening would have been slim to none. In fact, I would have stood a better chance of being one of the men in green at LCF, given my history, than where I am now.

Besides Still Waters

The cycling season was in full bloom in June of 2013, and Nate, me, and a group of cycling friends flew east for the HeartCycle Lake Champlain Tour. This one took us around northern Vermont and Lake Champlain. Starting and ending in Burlington, it took us to nine locations, including New York. It provided an opportunity to visit quaint towns off the beaten path and many historic landmarks and resort areas there in Vermont.

One of my nieces, Amanda, lived in Burlington at the time. In addition to taking me on a tour of downtown shops and, of course, eating establishments, she even tried her hand at piloting my tandem for a few miles before we bid her goodbye and soldiered on up through a fascinating historic pass called Smugglers' Notch. The Notch got its name due to an embargo President Thomas Jefferson imposed in 1807 to prevent American involvement in the Napoleonic Wars, which forbade American trade with Great Britain and Canada. Its proximity to Montreal made it a convenient trading partner, and the Act caused great hardship in the Vermont area. So, illegal trade with Canada was carried on through Smugglers' Notch. The route was then improved to accommodate automobile traffic in 1922, thus providing a route for liquor to be brought in from Canada during the prohibition years. Fugitive slaves also used The Notch as an escape route from America into Canada.

This pass was not what you would call an easy climb. There were a few stretches where the pitch reached 19 degrees, so Nate had the tandem in the granny gear the majority of the way. However, all was not hard work, as that leg of the ride took us close to where Ben and Jerry's ice cream was made. We figured finding our favorite would not be too hard: Chocolate Fudge Brownie. Given that Vermont was famous for its maple trees, we also had to try out the Maple Ice Cream. The next day, we rode sixty-seven miles, including a 5,700-foot climb that took up ten of those miles. We had ridden through torrential rain and roads covered with sand, which made all of us and our equipment a huge mess. So, when we had the following day off at a lovely local inn, it was a well-deserved two-day rest and an opportunity to dry out our soaked clothes and clean our dirty equipment.

When we arrived back in Burlington at the end of the tour, I spent a couple of extra days hanging out with Amanda. We shopped and ate great food, and she introduced me to kayaking on Lake Champlain. All in all, it was another great adventure with good people and my great God.

More Waters

HeartCycle then announced a new leg to the Great Adventure Tour for 2014, which was to be called the Great Rivers Tour. We would ride along the Mississippi River from Louisiana up to Minnesota, taking in a lot of Civil War history because our tour leader was a huge history buff, and he wanted to share his considerable knowledge on the subject with his cycling friends. History was my worst subject in high school because, at the time, it just did not seem to apply to me. However, as an adult who could now travel to all the places we merely read about in school, I found I was hungry to learn the important events that shaped our country, especially the Civil War.

Fortunately, God provided another pilot for me from San Diego: a tour leader for HeartCycle named Ken. We started out in March and once again faced bizarre weather, which was not unusual in that part of the country. We encountered snow and temperatures in the low thirties on the very first day. On the third day, we got our first history lesson, learning about how the Union Army of Tennessee under Major General Ulysses Grant gained control of the Mississippi River by capturing the stronghold there in Vicksburg. The history lessons continued daily after that, and it was not just Civil War stuff. In Tupelo, we visited the hardware store where Elvis Presley bought his first guitar!

The next day the weather got so bad it was not safe to ride, so we decided being "sagged" (transported by the SAG truck) to Lawrenceburg was the way to go. Little did we know that God would have to show up in a big way for us to continue. One of our SAG drivers, a Christian woman, was cruising along at about 60 mph on a wet road when, without any notice, a truck pulled out in front of our van. Thanks to her quick reactions, we barely escaped an accident that could have proved fatal to many of us. She swerved on the wet pavement but then brought our sliding Sprinter under control, just shy of going off the shoulder and down a steep embankment! Needless to say, some emergency prayers were going up at that moment, and the incident provided a lot of conversation around the dinner table for the next few days. The tour ended in Hurricane Mills the next day, where we would pick it up again the next year.

In April of the following year, I flew to Nashville, Tennessee, to begin the second leg of the tour. As was customary, we picked up where we left off the year before, and Nate Dick would be my pilot for the entirety of this tour. The majority of this leg would be over quiet country roads along the Tennessee River to its confluence with the Ohio River in Kentucky.

As we rode along, Nate would ask me how many dead people I thought were in the graveyards we passed by. Of course, this was a trick question because the correct answer is "everyone" (the mind does funny things to you when you exhaust yourself for days at a time).

Walking from our hotel over to the Gateway Arch in St. Louis on our next day off, we encountered huge Clydesdales hanging out in the street. We were able to pet them, and even with our arms outstretched, our hands did not reach the top of their backs. Though I had seen pictures of them as a kid, I did not appreciate what massive creatures they are until I got up close and personal with them.

From there, we rode along the Mississippi River to Mark Twain's (Samuel Clemens') birthplace. The next few days were filled with history lessons until we reached our final destination in Moline, where we enjoyed a group barbeque dinner at a place featuring the World's Best Twice-Baked Potatoes, and that concluded the Great Rivers Tour.

Potholes in the Air!

While this is a chapter about cycling, I could not let it go without my "airline nightmare" story; it seems everyone has one. Little did we know the most grueling and frustrating part of our tour would be flying home. Seven of us had purchased an expensive nonstop flight. We started boarding the plane at around 1:30 p.m. on Saturday. Thirty minutes later, our pilot told us we had to deplane because there was a mechanical problem that needed attention. They could not give us an estimate on repairs because the mechanic lived a good distance away from the small Moline airport. There was not much to do for a bunch of thrill-seekers to entertain ourselves. Boring!

Approximately two hours later, the agent at the gate informed us that the part the mechanic needed to fix the aircraft had to be flown in from Chicago, giving us a new departure time of 6:00 p.m. All those connecting flights we could have paid less money for were starting to look quite attractive. Oh, but the fun had just started! At around 5:00 p.m., we were informed our flight crew had exceeded their hours, so they would not be able to fly again until 6:00 a.m. the next morning. While the airline was gracious enough to put us up in a nearby hotel and give us meal vouchers, the only vendors who would honor the meal vouchers were the ones at the terminal, and they all closed at 4:00 p.m. One member of our party had sent all of her clothes home with the SAG truck, so she was stuck without a change of clothes.

By this time, everyone was pretty stressed out, and the thought of a good cold drink was on everyone's mind. After getting checked into the hotel, we agreed to meet at Montana Jack's for dinner and a few beers. Upon filling our bellies and sufficiently drowning our woes, we all returned to the hotel, knowing we would have to be up at 4:30 a.m. Sunday morning to catch our flight back to Denver.

At 5:00 a.m. Nate and I decided to walk to the airport for some morning exercise, but when we arrived at the airport, you guessed it, we discovered the flight had already been delayed thirty minutes. At 6:20 a.m. we boarded only to hear the pilot once more inform us the plane was still broken and our departure was rescheduled for 10:00 a.m. However, we were later informed that the mechanic had to drive from Milwaukee, which would take approximately 3.5 hours, so our readjusted departure time was now 3:00 p.m. that afternoon. How do they say it in the comic strips? AAARRRGGGHHH!

At this point, three of the group had had enough and successfully changed their flights to a connecting flight through Chicago. The other four of us headed back to the airport at 11:30 a.m. for some more vouchers and lunch. Then we endured our third security check, hoping the proverbial third time would be the charm. Sigh. However, it was not to be. Around 2:30 p.m. the gate agent informed us that once again the crew that would have been taking us back to Denver had, like us, spent the entire day at the airport and was once again out of hours! You cannot make this stuff up, folks.

The flight was canceled and rescheduled for Monday afternoon. This created a mob scene at the ticket counter, as passengers were frantically looking for an alternative flight back to Denver. Two members of our party got the last two tickets for connecting flights, which left just Nate and me still stranded in Moline. I thought someone should write a song—maybe me, as it appeared I had plenty of time to do so.

After spending the next hour working with customer service trying to find any alternative, we landed on making the ninety-minute drive to Cedar Rapids, where we could catch a flight at 6:00 p.m. back home. Nate scurried off to find a rental car we could book for a one-way trip. Nada. There we were, stuck in Moline. It seemed the next option was for us to hitchhike a ride to Cedar Rapids!

Then we got a break. As Nate was waiting to book our flight to Chicago, he just happened to overhear a woman talking about driving her son to Cedar Rapids so he could catch a flight from there. Nate put his considerable charm to work—motivated at that moment by utter desperation—and approached her. After explaining our situation to her, she talked to her husband and son, who were waiting out in their car. Praise God, she then let us know they would give us a ride.

When we arrived at the airport in Cedar Rapids a little after 5:00 p.m., we were informed that the flight that was supposed to depart at 6:00 p.m. would be delayed because of the weather. Nate figured that we would still have plenty of time when we arrived in Denver to catch the 9:20 p.m. bus to take him to Boulder, where his wife was planning to pick him up. After begging the captain of our flight to borrow his phone charger (Nate had left his in his luggage), the flight finally departed at 7:15 p.m. After arriving in Denver, Nate caught his bus to Boulder with a whole thirty seconds to spare!

The best part about this whole experience was that most of the time, the seven of us were there to keep one another company and make the best of the hand we were dealt. HeartCycle had turned us into a true family—a community that shared victories, defeats, and just life in general. In a society telling us we are to be rugged individuals and to work through life's trials by ourselves, God tells us we are to do it together. In fact, He says even the least of us has something valuable to give to the body, and without each member adding their piece, the whole body suffers. As independent as I am, I can always look back and know this blind man's story would not be complete without the many friends God has graciously placed in my life to help me along the way.

My Nostalgia Tour

In 2015, I was excited for a Washington/British Columbia Tour I had learned about, but, like always, I needed to find a pilot. I asked a young Christian woman named Lynn, whom I had met in my spinning class at the recreation center. She said she had never piloted a tandem before but was interested in giving it a try. We scheduled a day we could meet so I could show her the ropes. Not only was she a strong cyclist, but she was also very adept in the maintenance and repair departments. This came in handy when she had to break down my tandem, which was designed with couplers in order to fit it into a couple of suitcases for easier transport. Much as I was always willing to try out new pursuits, dealing with mechanical issues was out of my league, primarily because I could not see to diagnose issues, much less repair them.

Inasmuch as a group of us were flying Southwest Airlines to Spokane, my sister and brother-in-law were going to pick us up at the airport. There would be no problem with getting to know people on this tour! When introductions were made all around, my sister invited all of us to dinner at their house that evening so my friends could meet the rest of my siblings. When we arrived, Lynn, my sister, and my brother-in-law pitched in and had the tandem together in no time. Also, after my sister got a chance to know our two SAG drivers and find out exactly what they did on the tours, she and my cousin decided that they wanted to try their hands at it.

The next day as the tour began, Lynn and I found out quickly that mountain biking and road cycling are two very different skills. She was a mountain biker, and in her mind when a steep grade was encountered, you rose up off your seat and set yourself to conquering and powering through it. Encountering hills on a road bike, especially on a tandem, requires more finesse with the gears and less raw power. The first time we found this out was when she attacked a hill and broke the bike chain. After repeating this a couple more times, the tour leader and I were able to finally help her understand the difference between riding alone and piloting a tandem. Thankfully, we did not destroy any more chains after that.

All the memories on this "home" tour were special, but not as special as all the wonderful people I met on all the tours. On this one, I met a man named Tom from Parker, Colorado, who became a pilot for me on a couple of future tours. Then, a lady from Kansas and another from Ohio also became great friends. I shared my testimony with each of them, only to find out they already walked with Jesus. But that is the beauty of proclaiming your faith to others: you either find out you can touch a life for Christ or quickly connect through the Spirit to become good friends.

Out on the road, it was always fun to leapfrog each other and have fun competitions, with some friendly trash talk whenever the circumstances demanded it. We eventually passed by Christina Lake to another area I was familiar with from my past. Then we spent the night in Grand Forks before crossing the border into Washington, riding along the Kettle River, where I played as a kid. After spending a night in Republic, we headed back to Colville via Sherman Pass, the highest pass in eastern Washington.

Of course, I spent a couple of days in Colville before continuing my Nostalgia Tour as we headed to the coast of Olympia. At my cousin's house, we were joined by many friends and family for a memorial service for my Uncle Don and Aunt Jo. Yvonne flew to Seattle to join us. Once again, I was asked to speak, and I encouraged those present to consider where they would spend eternity because no one is guaranteed a tomorrow. When I got home from Washington, I called Tom to find out if he wanted to come over and try piloting my tandem. After just a few minutes of riding together, he told me that if he had known how much fun riding the tandem was, he would have volunteered a lot sooner! My meeting with him was one of those divine appointments that took away the constant burden of finding a pilot for my next tour.

Crisscrossing America III: Coast-to-Coast Tour

On the last Saturday of October 2015, it was back to the annual board meeting luncheon of HeartCycle. The director announced that they were going to complement the southern Great Adventure Tour with a ride across the northern United States starting in Astoria, Oregon, and ending in Portland, Maine. Once again, those who had completed the earlier legs would have the first option to register for this one. Of course, I had to search for someone willing to forgo a week of their comfortable lives to join the blind guy fighting the weather, fatigue, broken bicycles, crazy drivers, and to endure long, hard days pumping iron. No big deal, right? Any volunteers? Then I remembered my friend Tom and went back to him. He agreed to take one week, and Nate covered the other week.

During the summer months of the following year, Tom and I got out on the tandem a few times to get some training rides in for what I referred to as Coast-to-Coast Part Two that September. Several new cyclists had joined us because of no-shows from the prior tours. There are so many new opportunities for this blind guy to share his story! Another old face that joined us for this tour was Patty, still determined to "chick" Nate and me. She told us she had been working out for the past five years just so she could accomplish her goal, but we knew if it was going to happen, it would be by stealth instead of brute force, so we had to keep our wits about us and our heads on a swivel!

As it turned out, we were not the only ones sporting a tandem in 2016. One of the couples I got to know well was an orthopedic surgeon and his wife. The husband had once raced tandem bikes, where he and his partner took turns being pilot and stoker. He was such a strong rider that they were two of the few people who could actually beat Nate and me over most courses. Our meeting turned out to be another divine appointment, as he noticed I had poor alignment in my left knee and suggested surgery could help my riding considerably. This led to me getting both knees replaced over time. And you know what? He was right about it helping my performance on the bike!

As we rode, Nate pointed out to me that windsurfers were near Mount Hood. It reminded me of my ventures into windsurfing in this same area with my cousin and then with Yvonne during a Hawaiian cruise a long time ago. We enjoyed good weather until the day we were heading into Walla Walla, and the skies opened up! While the rain came down, Nate was able to pick up the famous CU/Michigan game on his smart phone because of his subscription to the CU Buffaloes App. Nate put his phone in a back pocket of his jersey so I could listen to the game where CU caught the second Hail Mary that won the game for CU. So the rain did not bother me one bit.

I was amazed by all the changes that had taken place there in Walla Walla since I was young. It was largely a farming community then, but now vineyards and wineries dot the countryside. Along with that, there were plenty of wine-tasting events taking place near the hotels where we stayed. Another chance to share my testimony over some really good bottles of wine!

Along one relatively flat stretch of highway, the other tandem couple and Tom and I played leapfrog, taking turns drafting off one another. For all the years that I had been cycling, everyone else loved to draft off the guys on tandem because we cut a bigger hole in the air than single cyclists did. This was the first time I ever experienced drafting off another tandem, which was a refreshing change! All four of us concluded that this was the most exhilarating and enjoyable time we had during the entire trip across America, averaging 22 mph on a 3 percent grade for over sixty miles! We smoked everyone else and were the first two bikes to reach our destination for the day.

This reminded me once again of our walks with God. So often, we try to take the lead and want God to follow us by "blessing" our activities. What we are really doing is riding into the wind, having to work much harder than we would if we would just let God go first and "draft" behind Him! Jesus said, "Come to Me all who are weary and heavy-laden, and I will give you rest. Take My yoke upon you and learn from Me, for I am gentle and humble in heart, and you will find rest for your soul" (Matt. 11:28–29). He loves taking the lead and having us follow. I have experienced both sides of this coin in my life, being a "getter-done" type. Trust me, life is much easier and the path to the goal much straighter when He leads and we draft!

The next day, we rode through a dense forest along the Lochsa River toward the Lochsa Lodge, an establishment rich in history dating back to the time of Lewis and Clark. My younger brother and his crew had built the Powell Ranger Station in that area several years earlier, so when I told him where we were, it brought back a lot of memories for him.

Like those two intrepid explorers, I did what a lot of men said was impossible. I ate three Huckleberry pancakes that were as big around as a dinner plate! Not quite so bold as Lewis and Clark, but hey, going where no man had ever gone before is the kind of challenge I like.

The following day, we headed up Lolo Pass on the way to Missoula, Montana, for our final day of this last leg of our tour. However, in the confusion of the pilot switch from Nate to Tom, I forgot all about our infamous stealth fighter "chick," who had us in her crosshairs and was just waiting to launch a surprise attack. (Can you just hear the "duhhhhh-duh" from the movie *Jaws*?) Then it happened: while Tom sat in front of me, keeping an even pace and whistling a favorite tune as though he did not have a care in the world, the attack was launched! Realizing my mistake, I started stoking as fast as I could, but it was all for naught. After five years of planning and training, Patty finally had her victory! I could only hang my head in defeat, while at the same time chuckling to myself as I reflected on this little competition that had gone on for so many years. After battling rain that turned to snow, we made it to Missoula and the end of the first leg.

In September of the following year, the second leg of the tour began with an unexpected blessing from God. The same orthopedic surgeon that I met on the first leg of this Coast-to-Coast Tour had been observing me ride and walk, and he recommended that I also have my right knee looked at when I got back to Colorado. He said he felt I could really improve my pedal stroke if I had both of my knees replaced. Only God watches out for you like that, revealing upcoming trouble before it becomes trouble.

Unfortunately, by the time we got to Yellowstone National Park, it was snowing heavily, so we did not get a chance to ride through on our bikes. That was a real bummer, not only for the sighted riders, but for me too. I was looking forward to all the sounds and smells I would experience riding through the park, as well as enjoying the thrill of the long descent into Cody, Wyoming. Instead, we were transported by bus into Cody. The sighted riders were still able to enjoy some of the scenery from the bus instead of on their bikes. The bus ride allowed me an opportunity to enjoy the scenery through more than just Nate's eyes, not to mention enjoying the like-minded company.

Then, it was on to Cody, Wyoming, where another pilot, Dave, was thrown into the lion's den. As soon as he started his leg of the tour, we faced a 100-mile day with a 7,800-foot vertical climb up the Big Horn. As if that was not enough, it began to rain not long after we started our climb. Then, one of the SAG trucks stopped to tell us it was snowing a little further on, and we needed to abandon our tandem and ride with them to Sheridan. While some of the single bikes could be loaded on the SAG, there was no accommodation for either of the two tandems on the tour, so we had to trust they would still be there when transportation was sent back to pick them up. Fortunately, we found a motel along the way that allowed us to wait for our bikes in their lobby while they served us coffee and hot chocolate.

Anyone who has driven through Wyoming is familiar with the constant winds that blow, and sometimes howl, from west to east across the state, and I could not help but wonder if Dave regretted his decision to be my pilot. Oh, and our mechanical gremlins were not done with us because someone damaged my derailleur when loading the bike onto the SAG truck. This issue cost us the last two days of the ride. However, we soldiered on to Rapid City, South Dakota, and the end of the second leg of the tour.

When I got home, I decided to follow up on the advice of the orthopedic surgeon to have my knee examined, and a friend from church referred me to a specialist that he highly recommended. I called the surgeon's office to set up an appointment and found I would have to wait for two months before he could see me. The knee did not prohibit me from getting around and did not cause me a lot of discomfort, so I felt it was worth it to wait for "the best surgeon."

The following year, we took off on the third leg of the Northern United States Tour in September, beginning where we left off in Rapid City, South Dakota. I wanted to make sure I got to the hotel in time to watch the annual CU/Nebraska football game that used to be played every year the day after Thanksgiving. That was back when they were in the Big 12 Conference and were both perennial contenders for college championships. It was a must-see TV (or, in my case, must-listen to) for anyone from either state.

On the first day of the third leg of the Coast-to-Coast Northern Tier, we rode through the Badlands of South Dakota, where we learned about the reservations of the Oglala Lakota Indian Nation. Like most reservations throughout America, these are depressing places with no opportunities, which results in no hope and a lot of drug and alcohol abuse. The weather was demanding, with strong winds as our constant companions, holding us up and wearing us down. There is accepting a challenge, and then there is "kicking against the goads." Nate and I decided we were doing the latter and got sagged into Sioux Falls. Our travels took us through Mitchell, where we checked out an actual castle built with corn stalks. Then we entered one of the longest legs, around 110 miles in a day, to Okoboji, where we would be rewarded with a much-needed day off. Fortunately, our old nemesis, the wind, took the next day off, and we were able to make good time for a change.

We stayed at a beautiful resort on a lake in northwest Iowa, where there were plenty of places for me to engage in one of my other favorite sports: eating! Then it was on to another 110-mile leg into Clear Lake. Guess who was back to torment us? The brother of Headwind, named Crosswind, brought the sand with him, and we all got sandblasted! However, Headwind was not done, for he had two cousins he invited to the party: Heavy Rain and Lightning Strike, and so our day was done as the SAG came and picked us up once more. I was beginning to have a whole new appreciation for the term Badlands.

Then it was on to Madison, Wisconsin, home of the University of Wisconsin. That evening, the riders joined up for a much-looked-forward-to happy hour at the bar. Because of all the excitement and celebration, I lost track of how much I had been drinking before I suddenly realized I had overdone it. Christians are not perfect, and if they are repentant and typically practice God's Word, there is grace abundant for them.

One of the traditions Nate and I had started on a tour ten years earlier was to always take Carol and Kathleen, our SAG drivers, out to dinner at the end of a tour. This was a way of showing them our gratitude for their exceptional kindness and assistance during our journey. As we visited with one another, I also had the opportunity to share my testimony with others sitting close to us. After a day off in Madison, we took a charter bus to Milwaukee, where we caught our flights back home.

I found out from Nate that he would not be able to pilot my tandem at all in 2019, so it was back to my new bionic knees in prayer to find another pilot to do the fourth leg of the tour with me. It was hard asking someone to take one week off to help me, but two weeks? Oh, me of little faith. My prayers were answered when a man named Jimmy, who had ridden tandem with his wife on some other HeartCycle tours, agreed to pilot me over the duration!

In April 2019, before the fourth leg of the tour, I felt the need to get a new and lighter tandem for future tours. I was not getting any younger and felt I needed to take any opportunity to make riding easier. I went to my favorite bike shop and found a bike that only weighed twenty-six pounds, which is nothing for a tandem. The problem with bikes is that the price goes up when the weight comes down—way up! However, because it was a floor model, we arrived at a reduced price of $10,000. That still seemed a huge expense, so before I decided, I had a local friend come over so we could take it out on a test spin. After putting a few miles on the bike, the decision was quite easy, and I ponied up the cash.

When I arrived in Grand Rapids to finish the tour, my shiny new tandem had already arrived, and I was told the other cyclists were drooling over it. I guess I did not realize what a gorgeous bike it was. All I knew was that it was light as a feather and, along with my new bionic implants, would make touring even more enjoyable. My first job at any event was to get my bike inspected and adjusted after shipping. Once we were on the road, the last thing we needed was breakdowns. This time, someone had improperly installed one of my pedals, causing it to be inoperable. We were forced to ride to a bike shop about six miles out of our way, with me pedaling with one leg. Fortunately, the technician at the bike shop was able to rethread the crank and properly attach the pedal.

After all the drama, the tour began with the goal of finishing up in Rochester, New York. We went through rural countryside, small towns, some big cities, and alongside numerous lakes and waterways. Our course took us through Michigan, then rural Indiana with its farmland and small towns. By this time, I had gotten my now-trademark "Son glasses," which always leads to more opportunities to give my testimony and invite people to make the most important decision of their lives.

Our next rest day was spent in Cleveland, Ohio, exploring the Rock and Roll Hall of Fame. Then, for the next three days, we traveled east on our way to Dunkirk, New York, where we spent a rest day under the spray of Niagara Falls. Then, it was a short two-day ride through the rural parts of the city to our final destination in Rochester. Little did we know we would not be back to that spot to resume the event until 2021, after the pandemic.

Steep Grades Ahead!

In the beginning of November, I rode the Tour of the Ozarks. Of the now thousands of miles I had put in on my tandem, this was the toughest event of them all. We arrived in Fayetteville, Arkansas, home of the University of Arkansas, where I met several new members of HeartCycle for the first time. Of course, meeting new cyclists meant more opportunities to share my testimony. My "Son glasses" never let me down in that area. On the first day, we rode forty-five miles through cool, drizzly weather to Mulberry Mountain, a resort in the heart of the Ozark National Forest. Then came several days of brutal 14 percent plus climbs, the worst being 22 percent. We were rewarded with a well-deserved day off at the historic Hotel Seville. I was blessed to have Tom, the pilot who had talked me into this grueling tour, as my pilot because he loved climbing.

Then it was on to the Las Vegas of the East—Branson, Missouri—where I looked forward to taking in a show. However, it was not to be because the leaders of the tour decided to avoid Branson due to the high automobile traffic that time of year. We ended up going to Little Rock, Arkansas, instead. From there we headed back to Fayetteville via a stop at historic Eureka Springs for a night. After that, we rode the last sixty-two miles back to Fayetteville.

At the HeartCycle Annual Board Meeting in October 2020, the announcement was made that the Covid-19 vaccine would be mandated for anyone planning to participate in any of the 2021 tours. I, like many others, objected to this because the Lord had blessed me with such a vibrant immune system; I rarely had a sick day my whole life. It had been over fifty years since I even had the flu, without so much as a single vaccination. I was not alone. Many objected due to what they considered an overreach of government control, as well as various other reasons. I hoped that perhaps by the time summer came around in 2021, they would drop the mandate, but that did not happen.

As the fifth and last leg of the Northern US HeartCycle Tour was looming in 2021, I finally gave in to being vaccinated for Covid-19, something I had zealously resisted up to that point. However, I just could not come that close to another traversing of America and call it quits. At this time, there were seven riders and two SAG drivers who had fully completed the previous twelve legs that crisscrossed the nation: the Ride Across America, the Border-to-Border, and the Great Rivers Tours. However, now I had two piloting needs to fill: the Northern United States Tour and an upcoming Italy tour I was excited about.

Nate had separated his shoulder during a spill in Oregon, so I reached out to a contact I knew in California. He was the director of a blind stoker club there, and he referred me to a young lady in Sedalia, Colorado, who then referred me to her boss, a guy named Scott. Scott was a cycling trainer/coach who taught young riders racing techniques. Although he had never piloted a tandem before, he said he would give it a try. After a test ride, he said, "Heck, yeah!" Scott was also schooled in the art of bicycle repair, which always came in handy. God knew the tandem would experience an inordinate number of issues on this tour and blessed me with a bike doctor who made house calls!

One of the things that impressed me about Scott, due to his racing training, was when to kick it into gear and when to "recover."

Rather than having me grind all the way up steep inclines, he would tell me when to stop pushing and enter a recovery phase of the climb so I would be fresher for the next push. I had never had a pilot who understood this, and it really helped me with my stamina over the course of the entire climb. Here, I thought I was the guy with all the grand touring experience and would be the one coaching the rookie. God has a way of humbling the proud.

As we got into New Hampshire, one of those mechanical gremlins caused the electronic shifter to experience a short circuit. We were dead in the water. We sagged it into town, and Scott and a local bike mechanic worked on it to no avail. So, alas, we could not ride the last few days of the tour, which was disappointing. It helped that on two of those days, heavy rain caused everyone to join us on the SAG truck. All you can do is your best, and Scott and I certainly gave it the ol' college try.

In Portland, Maine, we celebrated the end of the tour with a huge dinner of fresh-caught lobster to memorialize our accomplishment. You might have thought that finishing this thing was about pride of effort or something else more noble. Nope, it was about checking off one more item on my bucket list, sharing my testimony with hundreds of complete strangers, and developing some awesome friendships. I looked back with satisfaction, having ridden across America once more and accomplishing something, along with six other cyclists, that very few people have ever done. Did I forget to mention the great seafood?

I was informed at the HeartCycle Annual 2021 Board Meeting that they would replace me as registrar—a position I had held for fifteen years. This was disappointing to me because I was the one who had debugged most of their new software program using my IT skills. I got a lot of satisfaction from this position, as I felt it important to give back to an organization that had so blessed me. It was through the HeartCycle tours I was able to accomplish something no other blind person, I am aware of, and few sighted people had been able to achieve. Being one who never vested halfway in anything I did, this hurt because it seemed my efforts were not good enough. Oh well, I have to trust God on the mountaintops as well as the valleys.

Viva, Italia!

With tours being so rare at the time, I began scouring different websites to see what else, if anything, was out there. Lo and behold, I discovered one that had been on my bucket list for quite some time: a tour in Sicily, Italy, in 2022! My interest was to enjoy the cycling experience, acquaint myself with the culture, and savor the authentic foods in the region. Did I say how much I love food?

I registered immediately, thinking I would not have any issue finding a pilot for something so enticing and unique. The plan was to ride slower on the bike and take in more of the history and scenery than was the case with previous tours. Alas, finding a pilot for this tour turned out to be nearly impossible because, it seemed, no one wanted to fly halfway around the world during a global pandemic. Party poopers.

I finally got a lead. She was the daughter of my first pastor and the girl I rode to church with on my tandem many years prior. Jennifer trained competition cyclists and was a racer herself. I immediately called her, and she said she might be interested, or know someone else, who knew someone else, who … oh, you get it. Time passed, and nada. So, I called her again to see if she had heard anything. The bad news was that she had not. The great news was that she said if no one else stepped up, she would pilot my tandem herself! I was still hopeful we would find someone else because she had her own business, and a ten-day trip could seriously impact her bottom line.

After a couple of months went by, I started praying that somebody Jennifer was coaching would come forward and commit to going with me to Italy. A young man named Chris, who was one of her students, said the trip sounded wonderful, but he had already made another commitment. I felt the Holy Spirit nudging me to suggest to Chris that perhaps he could do some sort of fundraiser with Jennifer's class to support her being the pilot of my tandem. I contacted Chris and discovered he was praying about it as well, and the Lord was nudging him to organize a fundraiser for Jennifer. Another divine appointment!

Before Christmas, they had raised $4,600 to send Jennifer to Italy to pilot my tandem. Jennifer did not know about the fundraiser until just a couple of weeks before Christmas when, at their annual Christmas party, they sprung the whole plan on her, along with the check! When she opened the card and read the note, she was shocked to find Italy was suddenly on her travel plans. Some of her students joked that this was the only way they could get a break from her brutal training regimen, and everyone enjoyed a good laugh!

God showed me through Jennifer's story that I did not have the only rags-to-riches, comeback-from-injury-experience in this sport. We both had a farm upbringing in common; and she had blown out a knee fifteen years earlier, falling off a thirty-foot-tall haystack. We farm kids are tough as nails. To add to that, my new pilot had suffered a traumatic brain injury from a bicycle accident two years prior and worked her way back into form. At the time of the accident, Jennifer said she had an out-of-body experience. She found her spirit hovering over the scene of the accident, where she saw her unconscious body on the road. The woman who hit her later said it was otherworldly that Jennifer could describe the entire scene, including seeing the truck driver who called 911 from where she went down. It was impossible to explain how Jennifer could have seen it all.

Her younger brother, James, was the first person to pilot my tandem on my initial tour back in 1988 when he was fourteen years old and weighed ninety-eight pounds. Now, here was Jennifer serving me over thirty-four years later, as her brother had done, on what might be my last tour and first overseas one. Our working together required some adjustments to the tandem to make Jennifer comfortable and best suit her riding abilities.

On May 13, 2022, the big day arrived, and we caught our flight to Catania, Italy. As we checked in our luggage, we found the bike was now categorized as "oversized," though it had been shipped before and that was never the case. I had to pony up another $750 to get it there. God never promised us a rose garden. We joined up with nine other cyclists from Delaware who were fellow believers in the Lord. There is a special bond that exists when the Holy Spirit connects believers.

While I could not wait to sample Italian cuisine, Jennifer struggled to find anything gluten-free. Uh, pasta, pizza, and baked goods, anyone? This was gluten-free hell for her, and when you are expending the tremendous amount of energy you do riding a bike all day, you need serious nutritional intake. Fortunately for her, we did find a few restaurants that served pizza she could stomach.

Then I found out she was uncomfortable riding while taking her hands off the handlebar to grab her water bottle, and this led to dehydration and cramping. Together, the lack of nutrition and hydration made this dream trip more of a nightmare for Jennifer.

We had to take an extra day or two off for rest. Jennifer lost ten pounds, and I gained just as many.

While we were in Catania trying to return to the States, we ran into three problems: first, we could not check our luggage early, so one of us had to stay with the bags at all times. Second, there were no Covid-testing stations at the airport, so we had to find one at a local pharmacy outside the airport. Lastly, while she was able to get tested as I waited with the luggage, it would not be so easy for me to find my way out of the airport, get a taxi, find the pharmacy, and then repeat the whole process to get back! No big deal, right? Just ask for directions as you go without speaking the language. Yikes! Jennifer said she was concerned about all these obstacles, but I told her not to worry because this is something that I did all the time during my travels.

I had developed an absolute trust in God to get me to where I needed to be, and He was always faithful. This time was no exception. I met a lady who assisted me to where I could catch a taxi. Then the Lord directed me to a Swiss lady who spoke both English and Italian, and she helped me find an Italian taxi driver who spoke English. This taxi driver took me to the pharmacy, brought the pharmacist out to the taxi to administer the Covid test, drove me back to the airport, and escorted me inside the airport to where Jennifer was waiting with the luggage! Like I said, you just cannot make this stuff up, but God does it all the time. Chock up one more divine appointment! This was just one of many footprints-in-the-sand moments where God picked me up and carried me through a difficult situation I could not walk on my own.

Jennifer was more than a little impressed by the faith she saw in me. Doing all that without fear of being taken advantage of, robbed, or even mugged in a foreign country? The Bible has much to say about the concept of practicing our beliefs. When we routinely work out our faith muscles, we likewise get to see Him in action. Then, facing the hurdles of life becomes increasingly more comfortable. I am not saying life's circumstances are always easy, but Scripture tells us to pray, trust, and obey in all circumstances.

Those who do not practice faith have to move from crisis to crisis in fear because they are not sure whether God will show up. It is like any sport or profession: the more you practice, the more hurdles that used to bother you become opportunities to walk by faith. For the Christian, it is God who is in control, and He has promised to never leave us or forsake us.

Connections

If I had to choose, I would say the greatest reward of all the miles pedaled is not the satisfaction of having carried out something no one else may have accomplished or all the beautiful places I have been. Contrary to my kidding, it was not even the food. No, the best thing that has come out of my tours has been meeting and getting to know so many wonderful, fascinating people. I now have friends—many brothers and sisters in Christ—from all around the country. Like the store owner in Wyoming who noticed us shivering in the corner of his store, due to weather that had made the roads unrideable. He took us across the highway to his cabin with a wonderful big fireplace, where he built a roaring fire and made hot chocolate to warm us all up. So many more stories I could tell, but there simply is not room for them all.

I enjoy the many times my favorite question comes up concerning how I lost my sight, and I get to share my "blessing in disguise" response that led to me "walking by faith, not by sight." The Apostle Paul spoke of this when he said, "Be transformed by the renewing of your mind so that you may prove what the will of God is" (Rom. 12:2). Losing my sight forced me to either transform my thinking about what was important or give up in despair. Of course, my answer baffles some people because they do not understand what I mean by a "blessing in disguise." Naturally, when you cannot see, everything is in disguise. That opens the door for my testimony concerning my God of transformation, new vision, and second chances.

Many times after hearing my testimony, people say, "Man, you should write your story so more folks can hear this," and for many years, it was at the top of my bucket list. Then I met Michael Wolff through Ekklesia. I had tried to find a biographer in the past but did not have the considerable funds it would take to hire one nor any knowledge about how to get my book published. However, when Michael and I first met and I discovered he was an author, I was all over it! Imagine that.

When we stand before God to give an account of our lives, even those who say they believe, He will ask us how we spent those all-important "talents" He gave us (Matt. 25:14-30). What will truly count are the relationships we entered into and how we allowed Him to minister to them through us. Where we went, what stuff we accumulated, or any goal we accomplished in education, sports, or business will matter little if the relationships we were a part of, or failed to be a part of, bore no fruit for God's kingdom.

As of the printing of this book, I estimate I have ridden around 70,000 miles, two times across America, through virtually every sort of weather extremes, over mountain passes with grades exceeding 15 percent, flatlands that stretched for hundreds of miles, and everything in between. Moreover, while I am seventy-five years old and no longer cycling too far from home, I am still planning tours over several of the passes here in the Rocky Mountains of Colorado. This ol' body may not be what it was during my serious cycling years, but I am not ready to give up yet! Does anyone out there know of a good tandem pilot who does not mind a crazy backseat driver?

Chapter VI:

WHAT IS THAT SOUND?

In 1982 on one of our annual Lions Club blind cross-country ski trips in Snowmass, Colorado, a couple of friends of mine, Joe and LeRoy, and I joined some other visually impaired skiers from Phoenix at a favorite bar in Aspen for a few drinks and great fellowship. One of the skiers from Phoenix was a good friend of Joe's who exposed us to a sport I had never heard of before, yet it would play a pivotal role in my life for years to come.

The sport is called "beep baseball," and it was developed for the visually challenged. Joe's friend, Bill Gibney, played for the Phoenix Outlaws and was president of the National Beep Baseball Association. The sport was developed by one of the Telephone Pioneers in Colorado Springs in the mid '70s. The ball that is used is slightly larger than a regular softball and has an audio device installed in it that produces a loud beeping sound so the players can hear it rather than having to see it.

Later that summer we were able to purchase a couple of those beep baseballs and got a few other visually impaired friends together, along with some sighted volunteers, to play some recreational baseball with makeshift bases. We did this for a couple of summers whenever we could gather enough friends that wanted to play.

In 1984, my love for the sport took a big step forward when the Telephone Pioneers of Albuquerque, New Mexico, flew Joe, LeRoy, and me to the World Series of Beep Baseball being held in their home state. It was then that we learned the official rules for playing the game. The game consists of six innings with three outs per inning. Beep baseball is played with six visually impaired members, plus a sighted pitcher, catcher, and spotter. Each impaired team member is blindfolded to make sure no one with partial vision has an unfair advantage. There are two bases instead of three, first and third, and the batter does not know what base he will be running to until the ball is in play. Once the ball has been hit, the base operator will randomly activate one of the two bases, which will start it buzzing so the batter will know which base to run to, and the runner must make it there before the ball is fielded. The ball must stay between the two foul lines and cover at least forty feet. The ball is considered fielded when the fielder has the ball up off the ground and extends it away from his body. If the batter gets to the base before the fielder has control of the ball, it counts as a run. If the fielder has control of the ball before the batter gets to the base, then it is an out. Each batter gets four strikes and two pass balls. The pitcher for each team pitches to his own players and not the opposing team—the idea being to promote hits, not outs.

The three of us got so excited about competing at that level we decided to form a team back in Denver. It took us a while to scrape together enough players to get things rolling. Still, with the help of the Denver Telephone Pioneers and some awesome volunteers, we pulled it off and were able to compete in our first World Series Tournament in 1985 in Minnesota. We really had not had enough time, nor had we been able to gather enough skilled players to be very good, but it was a real win for us just to be there. Getting one run out of three games did not exactly get us into the playoffs. Still, it whet our appetites for the next opportunity to compete, which would be at the 1986 event in Palo Alto, California.

When we started beep baseball practice in the spring of the following year, we found a female pitcher who turned out to be very talented. We practiced twice a week to get ready for the upcoming World Series event, but first we had to qualify at the regional event in Topeka, Kansas. The folks at the national event did not want any more teams that could only score one run in three games. Party poopers. Anyway, the Regional Tournament was always the first weekend after Memorial Day, so that weekend became a time the team always looked forward to. Due to a lot more practice, some talented new players, and more experience in competitive events, we actually won the consolation bracket in Palo Alto that year. Not bad. This new Denver Beepers team improved from a one-run score in our first appearance at a NBBA World Series Tournament to winning the consolation bracket in just two years! However, at that World Series Tournament we ran into an A-bracket team named the Dallas Beepers. The similarity in team names motivated us to change our name to the Rocky Mountain Eagles.

In the summer of 1987, our beep baseball team went to Ithaca, New York, to compete in the World Series being played there. It was a miserable experience with temperatures that hovered around 100 degrees and humidity to match. The tournament itself was held in a park near Cornell College, where the teams stayed in the dorms. After the tournament was over, a huge party began, and I doubt the dorm was ever the same. After our celebration, it looked like a Category 5 hurricane filled with beer cans and bottles, pizza boxes, plastic cups and plates, and cigarette butts had blown through the place.

Despite the stress over my failed marriage to Mickey, I could not easily forget my responsibilities with the upcoming Beep Baseball World Series in Topeka in 1989. I was on the national board of directors, was the primary fundraiser for our team, a player, and the chief recruiter. Earlier that spring, I had recruited a couple of new players for the team, and I really needed to be around to support them so they would want to stay with us. This was one of several balls I had to juggle.

A "Rocky" Start

In the spring of 1993, when the Colorado Rockies first came to Denver, my involvement with the NBBA turned into something I had never imagined! I was at a men's breakfast when I met a gentleman who knew Roger Kinney, Director of Community Outreach Programs for the Colorado Rockies. He introduced us, and we got into a discussion concerning beep baseball. The suggestion was made that the Colorado Rockies might be interested in sponsoring the Annual World Series event if we could get it to come to Denver. The Rockies club was very interested in hearing more about my sport and how they could begin planning to sponsor the 1995 World Series here in Colorado.

I contacted certain critical members of my team to get their opinions, and they were all excited about the prospect. We put together a committee to assemble all the information required to submit a proposal to both the Rockies and the NBBA Board. Then, during our first meetings, we voted on a director for the Denver World Series effort and sent an open invitation to representatives from the Rockies to attend any of our meetings.

So many pieces would have to come together to make this inaugural Colorado event work, not the least of which was finding multiple connected soccer fields for the event, with a hotel nearby large enough to handle the participating teams from around the country. The hotel would also need a banquet room that could hold approximately 300 people and be able to cater our awards banquet on Saturday night at the end of the tournament.

After our proposal was completed and submitted to Roger Kinney with the Rockies, he met with their committee. He reported back to us that not only would they be delighted to host the tournament but they were also going to sponsor us with a $20,000 donation. Based upon our agreement with the Rockies, I put together a proposal to submit to the NBBA at that year's World Series held in Austin, Texas. Who said life is a bowl of cherries? If my experience means anything, it is a bowl of committees!

My duties never relented long enough for me to take a breath (self-inflicted chaos, one could say). In early June of 1993, our beep baseball team committed to attending one of the smaller Regional Tournaments in Hays, Kansas. The World Series was again being played in Texas, and we had learned our lesson concerning Texas and summer sports. We were able to muster five other teams, none of which wanted to go to Texas any more than we did. At the tournament in Hays, I received a special honor, winning the offensive MVP award with a batting average of .831! Eat my dust, Mickey Mantle!

Even though the Rocky Mountain Eagles would not be participating in the World Series in Austin, Texas, I had to attend the NBBA board meeting to present our bid for the 1995 World Series to be held in Colorado. Since I was in Austin, a Chicago team recruited me to play for them, which allowed me to kill the proverbial two birds with one stone. Once I received the blessing from the tournament committee, they presented our bid to the rest of the board, who answered with a resounding "yes!"

Now that the easy part was done, it was time to go to work and pull this thing off. We had to do considerably more fundraising and put together contracts with venues for everything from rooms to food, transportation, fields, etc. We also had to work with the city of Greenwood Village, where we decided it would all happen. Furthermore, I had to coordinate everything between the NBBA, the city, and the Colorado Rockies to keep everyone in the loop. Moreover, did I mention providing up-to-date info for all the teams coming to town? Of course, a lot of that responsibility fell on my shoulders because, well, in the words of Han Solo, "Hey, it is me." I just never knew when to quit signing up for anything and everything, but I looked at it this way: life was never, ever boring. It seemed the only ones who did not want a contract for putting up their twenty grand was the Rockies, and they will never know how much I appreciated that.

In August 1994, the Rocky Mountain Eagles finally made it to the championship game, albeit in the consolation bracket. We lost by two runs, but oh, how far we had come since that first miserable effort back in the '80s. That one was in Florida, and our hotel was right on the beach which, of course, presented an opportunity to test the seven seas I just could not pass up. (Are we sensing a theme here?) You guessed it, the king of "never-say-can't" almost drowned as I was caught by a dangerous undertow that threatened to pull me under. I never stopped to consider the warning signs because I could not see them. Out of sight, out of mind, as they say. Fortunately, I had learned through my devil-may-care life to always travel with others when taking on a new adventure, and two of my friends pulled me from Davey Jones' grasp.

Hosting the Big One

Then came the big day the following August of 1995 as our team and the Colorado Rockies hosted the first World Series of Beep Baseball to be held in our state. We were so very proud of all we had accomplished over the years, maturing from fledgling newcomers who could not score a run, to being in the finals of the consolation round, and now being the host city where all the other teams had to come if they wanted to compete. One of the perks of this was that a film production company called Becher's informed me they wanted to do a documentary about the event. They showed up at my house to interview me, followed me to the bus stop on my way to the field, and stayed to film practice. Finally, they captured the entire championship game on Saturday afternoon. The NBBA film garnered Becher's the Academy Award for Best Documentary of the Year!

However, it seemed my old nemesis, injury, could not leave me alone in this, my finest hour. We were playing a game with the Topeka, Kansas team when a ball was hit to the outfield where I was playing. Another fielder and I both dove for it, but we met head-to-head, resulting in "the indomitable one" getting seventeen stitches in the ol' noggin. We did not win the tournament, but we won that day. The next day, I was on the field playing ball, stitches and all. After all the hard work we put into that tournament, nothing was going to stop me from playing to the last out. This event and all the amazing people God brought together to make it happen will forever be a highlight in my life.

In August of 1996, it was back to Austin, Texas, for the World Series of Beep Baseball. The sad news was we lost on Friday and so were out of the dance, but the good news was I was free to head back home if I could find a standby flight. This would mean

I could attend Yvonne's birthday celebration for the first time since we got married.

Fast-forward to the summer of 2000, when the NBBA World Series was hosted by Taiwan, of all places. This was in response to the board sending a team over there to introduce the Taiwanese to the sport, which led to them sending a team to the United States for our World Series Tournament. Because of the expense of taking our Eagles there, we went to our biggest sponsor, the Colorado Rockies. They donated $12,000, and we were on our way. It was interesting to put up with the heat, humidity, and moisture in the ground at high tide, and the mosquitos that seemed to set up camp on our feet and ankles all day. However, the advantages of extending the sport internationally and the wonders of experiencing life halfway around the world far outweighed the disadvantages.

When the Major League Baseball season started the following year, I met with the new community affairs director of the Colorado Rockies to find out if they would be interested in sponsoring the 2003 NBBA World Series. I offered the same handshake agreement that whatever they donated over and above our expenses, would be returned to them—the same arrangement as in 1995.

When the Rockies agreed to that, I started my legwork once more to organize all the various entities and people to pull off another successful event. To my surprise, the city of Aurora had just developed a massive new sports park complete with all the fields we would need. Then, the Red Lion hotel nearby provided great transportation to and from Denver International Airport, buses to the fields, all the rooms we needed, and a great banquet hall and menu.

Then came the time to submit the proposal I and others had worked so hard on to the NBBA to host the 2003 World Series. As it turned out, the Rocky Mountain Eagles did not attend the 2002 event because our pitcher was in Florida helping his mother move into assisted living. However, as a board member, I needed to attend the meetings which were held during the Series. Once again, the Chicago team recruited me to play for them, so I got to enjoy the whole experience once more. I reflected upon the fact that I would never have known about beep baseball, much less experience the challenges and joys it brought to me, had I not been blinded.

My affiliation with the NBBA led to my affiliation with the Colorado Rockies, which in turn led to one of the highlights of my entire life. In 2002, the Rockies awarded me the Hal O'Leary Leadership Award, which was presented to me at a dinner held at Coors Field. O'Leary founded the National Sports Center for the Disabled, which sprang from his experiences with a group of disabled kids in 1970. Hal was a professional ski instructor when he volunteered to give a few of them a lesson. He was so touched by that experience that he formed the National Sports Center for the Disabled (NSCD). The center now mentors 3,000 participants annually in sports ranging from alpine and cross-country skiing to rafting, biking, and horseback riding.

The year 2003 arrived, and with it came the day my team and the Colorado Rockies once again hosted the World Series. The new soccer fields provided by the city of Aurora that year, the nicest we had ever played on, were a big hit with everyone. Ironically, I was not able to play because, as the director of the tournament, the bylaws forbade it. Over half of the players in our Rocky Mountain Eagles team that year were rookies, so we did not do well. Relegated to watching the games from the bench, the highlight of my tournament was getting clobbered on the forehead by a foul ball, which knocked me off the bench and onto my back. Fortunately, the incident did not inflict any severe damage and only served to prove to everyone how hardheaded I was. Later, a friend of mine, whose helmet had been split by one of my line drives a few years earlier, reminded me it was probably some sort of cosmic justice that I got beaned that year.

Betrayed!

God takes us to many mountaintops, such as the ones I had experienced at the Colorado NBBA World Series, but the valleys are always a part of the journey. The Lord never promises to remove those valleys, but He does promise to help us navigate them. I was about to crash into a valley that would wound me greatly. In 2004, the NBBA revealed an insidious side I never anticipated. When I was the director of the 1995 Tournament here in Denver, I had a handshake agreement with the Rockies to refund any part of their donation that was not spent directly on that event, back to their foundation for use in other charitable pursuits.

In 2003, I deposited the Rockies' donation into the NBBA charitable account, which was not mine to control. In a move I felt reflected poorly on me and the NBBA, the NBBA Board refused to honor my agreement with the Rockies to refund all excess donations. When I reported this to the Rockies, they told me they were not happy with me or the NBBA Board. Since this meant they would no longer support our team, and we could not make it on what I could raise alone, I figured it was time for me to hang up my cleats and end my association with the team I had founded over twenty years before. And so, 2004 was the last time I ever played beep baseball.

Chapter VII:

Other Aspects of Life

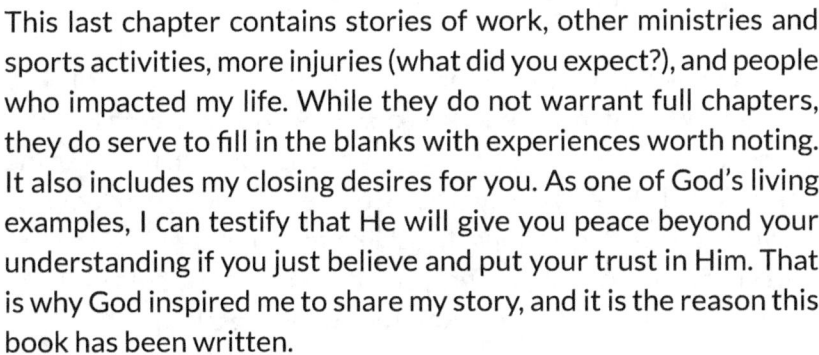

This last chapter contains stories of work, other ministries and sports activities, more injuries (what did you expect?), and people who impacted my life. While they do not warrant full chapters, they do serve to fill in the blanks with experiences worth noting. It also includes my closing desires for you. As one of God's living examples, I can testify that He will give you peace beyond your understanding if you just believe and put your trust in Him. That is why God inspired me to share my story, and it is the reason this book has been written.

That said, in 1981, I found myself out on the job hunt once more. I worked at a mortgage lending company, but because of soaring interest rates, that was a short-lived job. At the same time, I was collecting Social Security Disability Income, plus getting paid for my employment. After being gainfully employed for nine months, I was no longer considered disabled, so Uncle Sam stopped my SSDI payments at the same time I became unemployed. Ouch! I had to file for unemployment, but that would not last long since I had only been paying in to unemployment insurance for ten months.

I endured this circumstance for approximately seven months. It seemed like I had failed every job interview because no one understood how a blind person could possibly be a productive computer programmer. However, never being one to quit, I kept up the hunt. I was meeting with a Bible study group Bill Fay had put together, and it was there that I started to learn the power of fellowship. They gathered around me, prayed for me, spoke words of wisdom into my life, encouraged me, and supported me in many ways. They just kept saying, "Trust in God. He has a plan for you." Doing that was hard, having always been one who faced and conquered challenges on my own, and yet here I was, feeling powerless to do anything about this one. Little did I see at that time, God had me right where He wanted me!

My unemployment woes continued until early 1982. Bill Fay noticed it was taking a heavy toll on my relationship with Mickey. Through the struggles of my life, not least of which was being unemployed, Bill was always there to offer kindness, wisdom, and spiritual and physical support, just like Jesus did for His disciples. Bill sent me on retreats, his prayer group constantly held me up in prayer, and it was Bill who ultimately found me a job!

My Miracle Job

I finally gave up trying to count on myself to find employment and threw my arms in the air. I remember crying out, "Okay, God, if I need to put my trust in You, then You need to open up the door for the job they keep telling me You already have for me!" Shortly after that, Bill took my resume and handed it personally to a brother in Christ, Jerry Lewis of Petro Lewis Oil in Denver. Although the company had a hiring freeze in place at the time and thousands of other applicants more qualified than I was, I had an incredibly special agent working for me. Jerry took my resume and gave it to his human relations department. They called me in for an interview with the supervisor of their financial department, who handled computer programming. My guide dog Gordy saw his opportunity to help and went over and curled up on her feet.

Who could say no to the poor blind guy with the beautiful service dog that was chumming up to her?

Remembering my resolve to never work for oil companies or the government, this was the last place I wanted to be, but those desperate times called for desperate measures. Not only did I need the job, but I also wanted to get my foot in the door of proving to the world and myself, a blind programmer can be an asset to any company. They evidently saw my potential and offered to pay me $8,000 more than what I was asking! And so, on March 15 I officially became an employee of Petro Lewis.

I worked for Jerry until the oil crash of 1985. Petro Lewis was not immune to the troubles every other oil company was experiencing during that time. Jerry's company was set up as a private partnership rather than the typical corporate structure. When times got tough, many of the partners bailed, putting the company in a situation that forced Jerry to sell to a New Orleans-based group. Unfortunately, I was informed I was going to be laid off.

Captain Crash Strikes Again!

After reviewing my formal notice one morning, I needed to take Gordy out to mark his now-considerable territory. As I was crossing the street at a busy intersection, my old nemesis, injury, came to visit. A car roared out of a parking lot across the street and hit Gordy and me. When the ambulance arrived, they asked me where I wanted to be taken. I told them to take me to Denver General. Being more concerned with how Gordy was doing, I asked if someone would check him, but nobody in the emergency room would. So, I called a coworker at Petro Lewis, who took Gordy to my vet. Except for a few bruises and a cut on Gordy's tongue, it was decided he would be fine.

Gordy's diagnosis was moving along a lot better than mine, as I sat stewing in the emergency room for hours before they ever got around to taking X-rays that showed a broken thumb. They put me in a full arm cast, so I could not bend my right arm or use a keyboard. Great! Now, I was a blind, unemployed, one-armed computer programmer!

Because of the accident, Petro Lewis put me on sick leave until my arm healed. I was able to use this downtime to focus on finding new employment. Fortunately, that would not take long as the Director of the IT Department at Petro Lewis referred me to a contact of his at the Air Force Accounting and Finance Center. He gave me such a great reference, I was hired on the spot without being required to take a government exam. In addition to that, because of my education and work history, they hired me at a GS-11 level rather than the entry level position of GS-9.

Remember my resolve to never work for two entities in this world: oil companies and the federal government? So much for human resolve. Here I was being referred from the first entity I said I would never work for to the second entity I said I would never work for. I have learned if you want to do something just tell God you do not want to do it. I am not sure whether it is just His sense of humor or just an opportunity for Him to humble me. I was told to report to the new job as soon as I got the cast off. Turns out nobody from the private or public sector wanted to hire a one-armed blind guy to program their computers. Go figure.

There would be some time between my former job and my new one, so I decided to go home to Washington and attend a reception for my brother Roger and his new bride, who had just returned from their wedding in Reno. Aside from this brief interlude, my employment history did not skip a beat, and it became one of many indications to me that God was watching my back in every circumstance.

Finally, on March 31, 2010, my gainful employment ended. I showed up at the office to close down the files on my computer, turn in my badge, and, along with twelve others that I had worked with for years, walked out of the Finance Center for the last time. Then we all went out to breakfast to celebrate our retirement.

"RB" Hits the Slopes

In 1985, a group of visually impaired skiers and I were on our way to Snowmass in a large van. It just so happened another guy named Ron was sitting next to me during the trip, and it became very confusing to everyone because any time someone called out our name, both of us would answer. A young lady got the idea to call me RB when we went through an Arby's drive-through. That way people could have another name for me and call the guy next to me Ron. She said, "Ron Barton, your initials are RB, so we will call you "RB." For the seven days we were there at Snowmass, that was what everyone called me. It stuck, and to this day, I am still known as RB.

Through my newfound love for the slopes, my old friend, injury bug, bit once more in the fall of 1987, but that is what happens when a blind guy engages in activities that are considered dangerous even for sighted people. I returned to the Winter Park ski area for a new season on the slopes, facing the prospect of once again familiarizing myself with a new ski guide. I had been tired of that old rat race, so I thought I would let my stepson, Chris, guide me this year. We were on a trail that connected Winter Park to the Mary Jane ski area and were skiing side by side, holding on to each other's poles, when our skis got tangled up together. As we were trying to untangle on the move, Chris binding came loose from one of his skis, and he went down, jerking me off the trail and into a tree!

The ski patrol was notified, and when they found us, they told me not to move because they were concerned I might have broken my neck. They tied me up like a Christmas goose, put me in a sled, and took me to the patrol clinic to take X-rays. Unfortunately, they could not get a good shot of my neck, so they put me in a neck brace and called an ambulance. I had to ride on an extremely uncomfortable hard steel gurney all the way to Denver, where they could take proper X-rays. Chris was pretty shaken up and blamed himself for what had happened. I tried to reassure him that it was not his fault and that I still wanted him to be my ski guide, but he refused to go skiing with me again.

While my neck was okay, my left cheek did not fare so well. I cracked the cheekbone in several places, lost a couple of teeth, and broke my goggles, which in turn left a nasty gash in my eyebrow that left the skin hanging down over my eye. At least I did not have to worry about it further damaging my eyesight, right? Just call me "Mr. Silver Lining." Thirty-two stitches later, they put Humpty-Dumpty back together again. After that my dentist, Dr. Motzkus, decided he would start being my ski guide. We actually figured it out together and taught each other the best techniques for getting the job done. Without any formal training, the good doctor turned out to be the best guide I ever had!

In 1988 two visually impaired friends from Denver and I went to Snowmass for the Annual Lions Club Cross-Country Ski Event. Typically, there would be a guide for every one or two people to make sure the entrants stayed on the trails. However, the event was short-staffed that year, and because my friends were slower than I was, I decided to let them have the guide, and Gordy and I would go it alone. Part of the trail crossed a creek, over which was a narrow bridge the skiers had to navigate. A number of people typically fell from the three-foot-wide bridge and got soaked. There was a standing joke among the participants as to who would get baptized that year, whether they wanted to or not!

I am not sure if any other blind person had ever done that trail without a guide. Actually, I was not totally alone because my faithful friend Gordy was with me. I was relying on him to make enough noise so I could follow along. It was a no-no for people with service dogs to let them run free because they were so expensive to train, and it would be a disaster if one ran away or was injured. However, Gordy was very loyal and smart, and I was not worried about him running away. Anyway, this was one of the few times my impatience did *not* get me in trouble or hurt.

In February 1989, I registered again to race in the United States Association of Blind Athletes (USABA) giant slalom race, this time with Doctor Motzkus as my guide. It was held in Vail, Colorado, so at least it was nearby. I felt I did a lot better than in previous attempts, but I got disqualified during the time trials for skiing too erratically. Imagine that: me being out of control. Oh well, I thought, better luck next year.

It was a few years later that my love for both skiing and ministry expanded as I was introduced to Ski for Light (SFL), a group of volunteers that took skiers with various disabilities, not just the visually impaired, out on cross-country ski trails at regional events held around the country. They also had an international event each year hosted by different ski areas around the world. Breckenridge was one of these sponsors and committed to hosting the event every five years. People in wheelchairs were given specially prepared sleds attached to skis with short poles to push themselves along. Talk about commitment! Yvonne and I became involved in SFL, and we had a lot of fun learning to cross-country ski together.

When I attended the event in 1995, I found out I had been laboring for years on a pair of outdated, heavy cross-country skis. I met a man named John, whom I became great friends with; he introduced me to a lighter, waxable pair of skis, which increased my speed significantly. It seems I was better at going than stopping. The correct way to stop is to sit down on the backs of my skis, but when I failed to do this fast enough, I ended up crashing. Who, me? Crash? However, overall, the revelation of the new skis was a highlight of my year. John was also a highlight of my year, and we had a good time talking about the Lord. I never knew if the seeds I planted took root and grew because John died a few years later from cancer.

Later in the fall, I returned to the Regional SFL event held in Granby, and then onto the Lions Club cross-country ski event in Snowmass. Just another year in the life of the blind guy whom people were calling "the indomitable one."

In February of 1996, I traveled to Spearfish, South Dakota, to attend yet another International SFL event. The weather was miserable, with temperatures hovering around 20 degrees below zero. It was too cold to practice much, so we all spent the majority of the week, at least one hour per day, in the hotel, walking the halls to stay in shape. I thought I would rather die than walk one more set of stairs before it was all over. Talk about a root canal without Novocain! Not only was it tiring but also incredibly boring when compared to being outside practicing different routes in the snow and breathing the mountain air.

One of my favorite places to alpine ski was at Snowmass up on the Big Burn. What made it such a spectacular slope to ski was how wide, treeless, and open it was. It was one of the few places my ski guide would just let me ski at will, doing whatever I wanted to do while he just made sure I did not run off the course or run into another skier. It makes a lot of people uncomfortable to think of plummeting down a hill with no sight, but given time, you get used to it. The sound of the skis against the snow, the patterns you pick up in the way the moguls are spaced, the direction of the wind and how it hits your face, and the sounds of other skiers all combine to help you know where to turn and where you can go straight. Oh, did I forget to mention a good ski guide?

During the spring of 2001, I went to our Regional SFL event and also to the Lions Club Cross-Country Ski Event in Snowmass. Then, in 2003 and 2004, I was honored to receive another type of award for doing nothing more than what God wanted me to do. I was presented with consecutive Humanity Awards by the Sertoma Club, a century-old organization with a mission of meeting the needs of communities through volunteer service. The rewards acknowledged what they called outstanding work in our community here in the Denver metro area. I cannot take credit for any of it. Oh yes, I was obedient when God prompted me, but His Spirit was the inspiration and motivation for it all. In my prior life before the loss of my sight, I was not into helping anyone but "number one." However, after I met Christ, it became for me as the Apostle Paul said, "It is no longer I who live, but Christ who lives in me and the life I now live in the flesh, I live by faith in the Son of God" (Gal. 2:20). It is God who gets all the credit.

Ministering to Our Kids

Prison ministry was not the only ministry pursuit I was involved in at that time. Deciding I did not have enough to do in life in 1996, I took Pastor Tom up on his request for volunteers to help at a place called the Prodigal Coffee House. This was a safe place for runaways and homeless youth that was in the very same building Bill Fay, the man who introduced me to Christ, had used as a house of prostitution before his conversion. I went down with the pastor on a Thursday night and met one of the other volunteers, Jeff Johnson. Jeff played in a country band and directed an effort called Mile-Hi Ministries in Denver for many years that reached out to people like the ones we saw at the coffee house and more. He and I ended up playing our guitars together as a way to connect with those kids, in hopes of drawing them off the streets.

At Thanksgiving and Christmas, the church put together dinners for these kids and got them gifts. As I got to know more of them personally, I understood where they were headed if they did not change the direction of their lives—probably to prisons like Fremont, where I ministered to adult inmates. My hope and my goal were to guide these kids in making correct choices now so I would not be ministering to them later in prison.

I invited Yvonne to come down and meet the kids, and after she did, she confessed she found it hard to love them with their tattoos, rings stuck everywhere in their bodies, and the black face cosmetics and dress so popular with the Goth culture. I smiled and reminded her one of the great blessings of my blindness was that I did not see what was on the outside, which left me free to concentrate on what was on the inside.

When you think about it, how many people do we shy away from or "profile" in our mind because they are overweight, of a different color, dirty, unkempt, tattooed, or dressed in a manner that seems ridiculous to us? Because of that, how many do we write off without hearing their stories? On the other hand, how many people with little substance or integrity are revered and made famous just because they are beautiful on the outside?

This was a vital part of my "walk by faith, not by sight" blessing. Being physically blind sets me free from prejudiced opinions based on external appearances and allows me to really hear what is in their hearts. I try to "read" people through what the Spirit is telling me.

One memorable event with the kids at the coffee house was when we tackled a rope course and zip lines adventure. The kids were always intrigued that I participated in all the various activities with them. One of the most difficult parts of this trip was to climb up a tall pole and then stand on the very top of it. From there, we had to jump out and try to catch a trapeze bar hanging about nine feet away. As they all gasped, I took the plunge and missed the bar, but all was good because I was hooked up to a security harness!

Anyway, the kids just could not understand why I seemed fearless, given my blindness, but this always opened up opportunities for me to share the Lord with them. After some cajoling from the blind guy, two of the kids overcame their fears and were able to climb that pole, jump out, and catch the bar. What a topic to talk about during the Bible studies they were required to attend in return for all the fun: God is our security harness! Though He often asks us to jump off our poles of comfort, across chasms, and into the unknown, if we will just take the leap of *faith*, He is always there to catch us if we fall. In fact, He would much rather catch someone who stepped out in faith and fell than not have to catch someone who did not have the faith to jump at all. Thinking about my youthful years, though we had our disagreements, my parents stuck together as a couple and loved their children unconditionally.

A Different Skiing Adventure

In August of 1998, I was reacquainted with a sport I had not been involved in for over twenty-five years: water skiing. One of my nephews and his wife lived in Sacramento, which is where the NBBA World Series was being held. After the tournament was over, I was able to spend a couple of days with them, and they took me out on their boat. It was definitely a different experience than my last one because back then, I still had at least some sight left. Nevertheless, water skiing was a lot of fun because there were not too many trees or people to run into like there was on snow.

Puttering Around

Fast-forward to April of 2021. At one of our Narrow Gate Men's Fellowship luncheons, Bo announced the annual Narrow Gate Golf Tournament that would be held in May and asked whoever wanted to play to register. I jokingly asked if they accepted blind golfers to play in the tournament. Bo graciously told me I could, so I signed up, although I had never held a golf club in my life. The tournament would be a four-man shuffle, and knowing I had played beep baseball and was like a homing pigeon when I got anywhere near a location I was familiar with, Bo asked me to be the designated putter on his team.

Our foursome consisted of me, Bo, a man named Lee, and the lone woman in the tournament, Susie. Lee took on the duty of being my spotter, taking me out onto the putting green, where we came up with a numbering system of how hard I needed to hit the golf ball to reach the hole. Then, he talked me through the topography of the putt and help me line it up to navigate that part of it. Believe it or not, I was voted the MVP of the tournament, making 85 percent of my putts! You never know until you try.

The End of My Story?

This story, the biggest item on my bucket list for years, now comes to an end; but my journey with my God, who is always doing a "new thing," has just begun! This servant of Jesus Christ will continue to follow the One who saved me and walks with me with all my heart, soul, and mind. I will go on sharing my testimony that I was blind, and it took the loss of my eyesight before I could see. I have learned to "walk by faith, not by sight"; I hope my story will inspire you to do the same.

I pray this book will allow me to reach a wider group of people and inspire readers to "forget what lies behind and reach forward to what lies ahead" (Philippians 3:13). I pray you will be encouraged by these verses: "you can do all things through Christ who strengthens you" and "press on toward the goal for the prize of the upward calling of God in Christ Jesus" (Philippians 4:13). We serve a God who never retires His warriors. There is always and forever the next level, and that is what still, at the age of seventy-five, wakes me up every morning with a smile on my face and a reason to get out of bed.

I am reminded of the Apostle Paul's statement in Philippians 1:21–24, "For to me to live is Christ, and to die is gain. If I am to live in the flesh, that means fruitful labor for me. Yet which I shall choose I cannot tell. I am hard-pressed between the two. My desire is to depart and be with Christ, for that is far better. But to remain in the flesh is more necessary on your account."

Being the evangelist that I am, all I can hope is that this story of my "Son glasses" will open the eyes of those with whom I get to share the good news of Christ's love. Being the disciple my biographer and friend Brother Wolff is, he also prays this book will encourage believers to live out their faith. We hope what you have read here will cause you to seek a deeper and more meaningful relationship with Jesus Christ.

Since we started working on *Son Glasses*, Michael has also become a valuable member of Ekklesia Prison Ministry, bringing his unique perspectives on faith, the church, and the kingdom to our brothers at LCF. Now, like so many relationships that begin when the Holy Spirit teams up two people, we look forward to what God has for us as a team moving into the future.

I hope the one-two punch of evangelist/disciple God put together when He united us to do this project will provide a well-rounded and powerful witness as to what Jesus Christ can do in your life, if you will just submit your will to Him and allow His Spirit to guide you. We will both close by saying, "God bless you and keep you and make His face to shine upon you as you travel the path He guides you on! Shalom, brothers and sisters."

Appendix:
Is It Time?

You have now seen the amazing things God can do with just one man who believed and spent a life acting on those beliefs. How about you? Is it time to consider where you stand with Jesus Christ and make a decision either to invite Him into your life or recommit to following Him in deed and in truth. If you want to become a Christ-follower or truly renew your commitment to being a Christ-follower, we invite you to review the following passages that speak to both.

There are wonderful parachurch ministries everywhere that you can plug into. For me (Michael), it was Young Life. For RB, it was Kairos, now Ekklesia. Seek God's path for you until you find it! If you need help with a stalled walk of faith, we hope you will go to Michael's website: www.TheAwakenedChristianman.org, and check out the resources there, all designed to help you deepen your relationship with Christ.

In addition, here are a few recommended websites that will serve to guide you:

https://www.bibleproject.com/
https://peacewithgod.net/
https://peacewithgod.net/topics-questions/
https://goingfarther.net/
https://goingfarther.net/article-categories/

https://billygraham.org/
https://billygraham.org/grow-your-faith/

Passages to Think About

Romans 6:23—"For the wages of sin is death, but the gift of God is eternal life in Christ Jesus our Lord."

Romans 10:9—"If you confess with your mouth that Jesus is Lord and believe in your heart that God raised him from the dead, you will be saved."

John 3:3 —Jesus replied, "Very truly I tell you, no one can see the kingdom of God unless they are born again."

John 14:6—Jesus answered, "I am the way and the truth and the life. No one comes to the Father except through me."

Ephesians 2:10—"For we are His workmanship, created in Christ Jesus for good works, which God prepared beforehand so that we would walk in them."

Matthew 6:33—"Seek first His kingdom and His righteousness and all these things will be added to you."

Matthew 28:19-20—"Go therefore and make disciples of all the nations, baptizing them in the name of the Father and the Son and the Holy Spirit, teaching them to observe all that I commanded you."

Romans 12:1-2—"Therefore, I urge you, brothers and sisters, in view of God's mercy, to offer your bodies as a living sacrifice, holy and pleasing to God—this is your true and proper worship. Do not conform to the pattern of this world but be transformed by the renewing of your mind. Then you will be able to test and approve what God's will is—His good, pleasing and perfect will."

Philippians 2:13—"For God is working in you, giving you the desire and the power to do what pleases him."

A Prayer to Pray

Ron and I (Michael) want more than anything to see you begin or recommit to a new life with Christ. We want your commitment to be real and your life as exciting and rewarding as the one you have just read. Knowing Jesus and how to serve Him is a lifelong journey with eternal rewards. If you are ready to start that journey, pray this prayer:

"Lord Jesus Christ, I believe You are the Son of God. I believe You came to earth as a man and that You were crucified and shed Your blood as God's Sacrificial Lamb. I believe You rose from the grave, conquering the power of sin and death. I confess that I am a sinner, and I repent of the sin and pride in my life. Come into my heart now and be my Lord and Savior. I ask for Your Spirit to guide me as I walk, Your grace to uphold me when I stumble, and for the realization that I am a new creation and Your beloved child from this day forward."

ABOUT THE AUTHOR

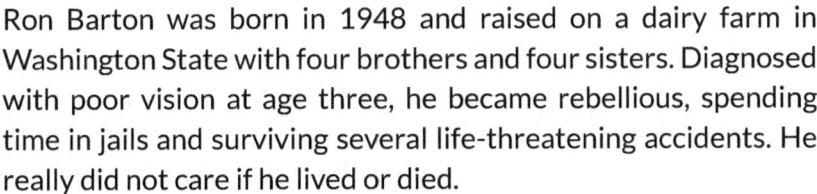

Ron Barton was born in 1948 and raised on a dairy farm in Washington State with four brothers and four sisters. Diagnosed with poor vision at age three, he became rebellious, spending time in jails and surviving several life-threatening accidents. He really did not care if he lived or died.

In 1973 Ron would embark on what was supposed to be a two-week vacation, a journey that would change the rest of his life. In 1975, during a mugging at a bar in Colorado, a blow to his face would take his sight. Unbeknownst to him, this seeming tragedy would cause a total transformation of his life.

Wherever Ron travels he always looks forward to being asked about his blindness. As he shares his story, he gets the same response, "you need to write a book." Read on and then you will know, as Paul Harvey would say, "the rest of the story!"

Ron attends Cherry Hills Community Church in Highlands Ranch, Colorado, and is living in Centennial Colorado with his wife Yvonne and his service dog, Nicolina.

www.ingramcontent.com/pod-product-compliance
Lightning Source LLC
Chambersburg PA
CBHW062319120626
46546CB00013B/2097